About the Author

Michael Furie (Northern California) is the author of *Spellcasting for Beginners*, *Supermarket Magic*, and *Spellcasting: Beyond the Basics*, all published by Llewellyn Worldwide. He has been a practicing Witch for more than twenty years and is a priest of the Cailleach. You can find him online at www.michaelfurie.com.

To Write to the Author

If you wish to contact the author or would like more information about this book, please write to the author in care of Llewellyn Worldwide, and we will forward your request. Both the author and publisher appreciate hearing from you and learning of your enjoyment of this book and how it has helped you. Llewellyn Worldwide cannot guarantee that every letter written to the author can be answered, but all will be forwarded. Please write to:

Michael Furie
⁒ Llewellyn Worldwide
2143 Wooddale Drive
Woodbury, MN 55125-2989

Please enclose a self-addressed stamped envelope for reply,
or $1.00 to cover costs. If outside the USA, enclose
an international postal reply coupon.

A Magical Year Using Everyday Ingredients

SUPERMARKET SABBATS

MICHAEL FURIE

Llewellyn Publications
Woodbury, Minnesota

First Edition
First Printing, 2017

Book design by Bob Gaul
Cover design by Ellen Lawson
Cover illustration by Anne Wertheim
Editing by Laura Graves
Pentagram art by Llewellyn art department

Llewellyn Publications is a registered trademark of Llewellyn Worldwide Ltd.

Library of Congress Cataloging-in-Publication Data
Names: Furie, Michael, 1978– author.
  Title: Supermarket sabbats: a magical year using everyday ingredients / Michael Furie.
  Description: First Edition. | Woodbury: Llewelyn Worldwide, Ltd., 2017. | Includes bibliographical references and index.
  Identifiers: LCCN 2017015202 (print) | LCCN 2017035168 (ebook) | ISBN 9780738738710 (ebook) | ISBN 9780738751016 (alk. paper)
  Subjects: LCSH: Sabbat. | Religious calendars—Wicca.
  Classification: LCC BF1572.S28 (ebook) | LCC BF1572.S28 F87 2017 (print) | DDC 133.4/3—dc23
  LC record available at https://lccn.loc.gov/2017015202

Llewellyn Publications does not participate in, endorse, or have any authority or responsibility concerning private business transactions between our authors and the public.

All mail addressed to the author is forwarded, but the publisher cannot, unless specifically instructed by the author, give out an address or phone number.

Any Internet references contained in this work are current at publication time, but the publisher cannot guarantee that a specific location will continue to be maintained. Please refer to the publisher's website for links to authors' websites and other sources.

Llewellyn Publications
A Division of Llewellyn Worldwide Ltd.
2143 Wooddale Drive
Woodbury, MN 55125-2989
www.llewellyn.com

Printed in the United States of America

Contents

....

....

Section 3: Summer Surge

....

Section 4: Autumn Harvest

....

CHAPTER 1

Basics and Background

Every year, usually in the third week of September, one of my most joyful shopping experiences occurs: the day I walk into the local grocery store and spot them—the overflowing abundance of pumpkins! I adore Halloween, and Samhain is my favorite sabbat. Seeing the displays always signals the beginning of my favorite time of the year. As pumpkins have become a staple crop of Halloween and the carved jack o' lantern can be used as magical protection, they are a perfect example of a seasonal item packed with magical potential that most people buy from the supermarket. After that, at least in the United States, Thanksgiving adds new products and the holiday season lends even more specialty vegetables, fruits, and other items to the usual grocery store inventory. Pick any time of year and the store is chock-full of things particular to that season, most of which a magically minded person can use in their practice to attune to the seasons, celebrate the sabbats, and create change.

In most supermarkets, particularly in the United States, the standard "mainstream" holidays—New Year's Day, Valentine's Day, Saint Patrick's Day, Easter, Independence Day, Halloween, Thanksgiving, and Christmas—are usually represented in some fashion. Decorations, specialty foods, and beverages in colorful, carefully arranged displays (probably meant to encourage maximum impulse buying) fill the aisles and create a sense of continuity. At first glance this purchasing advantage does not seem to be equaled for Witch and Pagan holidays, but with a keen eye and careful shopping, we can find that all of our festivals have representation in the supermarket.

Many people might overlook the local grocery store when seeking magical ingredients, but it is actually a treasure trove of power for both spellwork and holiday celebration. Our modern stores have become international marketplaces that provide spices, herbs, and foods from all over the globe, each of which have magical significance. Exotic, hard-to-find ingredients are not the only ones with power, however; even the most "ordinary" items contain magical potential. And therein lies the strongest virtue of supermarket magic: readily accessible ingredients can provide a complete resource for our spells, holidays, and witchy crafts.

At first glance, it might seem that the creations made from such simple ingredients might not result in powerful magical formulas, but between the basic herbs and spices and the advantage of the special seasonal offerings that become available, powerful concoctions such as Ancestor oil, Faery Dust powder, Fire Dragon oil, Bubbling Love potion, and many more can be made with ease. The sabbats too can find their accoutrements straight from grocery store shelves—oils, powders, potpourris, foods, and a whole host of magical creations are possible for each special day, providing a rich holiday experience all without having to hunt down fabled, rare, or endangered ingredients. An ordinary trip to the supermarket is transformed into a quest for the makings of magic.

Witches and other magical people often try to live in tune with the earth and the seasons, but in the modern world it is often easier said than done. With the incredible resources we have at our disposal in the form of supermarkets, we can still follow the cycle of seasons albeit in a modern capacity. Even though many of us no longer grow the food we eat, we still maintain a connection and dependence on the earth's yearly agricultural and seasonal cycles. Putting modern industrialized farming practices and importing of produce to maintain yearlong supplies of seasonal foods aside, we can still make a conscious choice to live seasonally as best we can and carry on the traditions of establishing a personal connection with the fruits of the earth. Some of us are blessed with the land and talent to grow our own Witch's gardens with fragrant herbs and magical delights to enhance our spells and provide us with a firm grounding in the energies of the earth. Even under those circumstances, however, it's nearly impossible to grow everything a Witch would need for a well-rounded practice.

With the rise of Internet shopping, we now have the opportunity to purchase rare or exotic herbs from all over the world through the magic of a credit card and the click of a mouse. Many of us have chosen this option to stock our herb cupboards with the items needed to craft our oils, powders, and brews both for our spellwork and for our sabbat celebrations. This option can be time-consuming and pricey (especially with shipping and handling charges) and is not really practical as the only source for our magical ingredients. In my personal practice, I have tried to focus almost exclusively on herbs and items that are readily obtainable from supermarkets for four main reasons: gathering ingredients in this way is much less expensive than other options; getting herbs from the supermarket means I am not helping to deplete rare or endangered species of plants in the wild; it is so convenient to have what I need available at most nearby stores; and my magic remains just as successful with these simple ingredients as it has been with rare, exotic herbs, roots, and resins.

Kitchen witchcraft, as it has come to be called, is really an exercise in magical practicality and making the most of what's available to us at the time. Some of the most powerful magic I have seen has come from Kitchen witchery. Did you know that there is an ancient method of protecting pets and other animals from mischievous or malevolent faeries that can be made from a few simple ingredients? Or that a formula can be cooked up right on your kitchen stove to call forth the presence of sea sprites and even the energy of the mystical mermaid? In one of my previous books, *Supermarket Magic*, it was my goal to show that magic is everywhere and that we can access rich sources of energy and power right from our local markets, using these tools and ingredients to cast spells and enchantments to achieve specific goals. With this work, it is my intention to demonstrate how easy, practical, and fulfilling it can be to expand the kitchen magic into a broad practice that encompasses the sabbats, esbats, and seasons to create a wonderfully complete spiritual experience.

As in my previous work, there will be lots of things to make and do, so it is sensible to go over the basic preparation methods of these items in this chapter rather than repeat steps over and over throughout the book. In the recipes presented, I have chosen to include in parentheses the reason for the chosen ingredients. Since many herbs and foods have multiple magical correspondences, I thought it might be helpful to clarify what specific energies you will be drawing.

Charging with Intent

In order to properly align and focus the energies within an item or spell ingredient and fill it with your magical goal, it is important to charge it with your intention. Doing this can be as simple as holding the item or placing your hands over it, mentally willing your energy to flow while visualizing that your energy moves over and into the item(s) in a sun-wise circular motion as you say this or something similar:

> *I neutralize any energies not in harmony with me,*
> *And charge this [herb, tool, etc.] with*
> *[state intention] power.*
> *For good of all and by land, sky, and sea,*
> *The energy is fixed; as I will, so mote it be.*

The tools or ingredients can now be used in your magical workings.

Preparing Simmering Potpourris

These are made by simmering the mixture of herbs and water in a pot on the stove so that the rising steam scents the air to creates the appropriate atmosphere. Grind the herbs together in a bowl and mentally charge them with your energy and magical intention before adding them to the pot of water. Simmer on the stove so that the mixture begins a light boil and starts to release steam. You could also use a slow cooker instead of a pot on the stove for a longer effect.

Preparing Brews

Double, double, toil and trouble! This process is quite easy. Hold the individual herbs in your hands and charge them with your intent, then put them in a pot (a cauldron is ideal), pour the necessary amount of water over them and simmer over low heat for about 10 minutes or so until bubbles form at the bottom of the pot and steam is rising; the water should not reach a rolling boil. Next, remove the potion from the heat, cover, and allow it to cool for about another 10 to 15minutes. When cooled, strain and sweeten if necessary or desired. The potion is then ready.

Preparing Incenses

In my previous work, I chose to omit incense recipes, feeling that in a book aimed at using ingredients exclusively from the supermarket, it didn't make sense to include raw incense formulas that would need to be burned on the specialty charcoals that cannot be found in a grocery store. For this book, however, I am reversing my opinion on the matter; cauldrons, chalices, athames, and wands aren't usually found at these stores either, but I am still recommending their use. The proper charcoals can of course be purchased online, at Witch shops, or in many religious bookstores.

To create the incenses, simply grind each herb, charge with your intent, and combine them together. Next, add whatever liquid ingredients are called for in the recipe (if any), charge the completed mixture once more, allow to air dry if needed, and bottle for use.

Preparing Magical Oils

To begin, gather the ingredients and a pot, spoon, strainer, and bottle for the finished product. Grind the herbs in a small bowl with your fingers (or use a mortar and pestle if necessary), mentally pouring your magical intention for the completed oil into the herbs to charge them. Once the herbs are charged, sprinkle them into the pot. Then pour the proper amount of oil (amounts are given in each recipe) over them and swirl the pot to blend the mixture. Warm the oil over very low heat, stirring slowly until you can smell the scent of the herbs in the air. At this point, remove the oil from the heat, and allow it to cool. When it has cooled, strain the oil into a jar. This is the basic procedure. Any alterations (if needed) will be given within that recipe.

Preparing Powders

To create a magical powder, all that's required is to grind each individual herb with your hands, a mortar and pestle, or a coffee grinder (preferably not one you use for your daily pot of joe!) and then place them in a bowl. When all the herbs have been added, mix them together with your fingers, charge the completed powder, and bottle for use.

Preparing Vinegars

This is a simple process of charging the chosen herbs with your intention and adding them to the vinegar, bottling the mixture, and keeping it in a cool dark place for about a week to infuse the essence of the plant materials into the acidic vinegar. The bottle can be swirled or lightly shaken on a daily basis to help the process along.

Any of the other magical creations will have their instructions listed individually since their methods will vary.

Magical Essentials

It is safe to assume that anyone drawn to this book has an understanding of magic, but since magical practices can be so varied, I will include some of the basics as I have come to understand them. The first two components of successful magic are intent and feeling.

Intent

This is the clearly focused vision of what you are trying to accomplish; the magical goal. When working positive magic, it is best to have a fully formed concept of what you wish the outcome to be while at the same time not dwelling on the process of how you might think the goal "should" be reached. Thinking about the process can delay manifestation of your intent by placing unnecessary conditions upon it; focusing only on the goal allows for greater freedom of action.

Feeling

The most vital factor in magic as far as I am concerned is infusing into your intent the way you wish to feel when the goal is reached. Doing so channels the energy in such a way as to manifest your goal without undue stress or problems and helps to eliminate that "be careful what you wish for" problem.

Working for the Good

Another method of minimizing potential magical mishaps is making sure that all your workings are done with the idea that the magic occurs "according to free will" and/or "for the good of all" or "for the highest good" or "with harm to none". This will include in the magical intent the condition that when the goal is reached, it will not be because of any coercion, manipulation, unfortunate incidents, or harmful situations. This can be stated at the end of spells or merely held in the mind as an underlying concept. It is a given that the spells in this book meant to affect another should be used with this guideline in mind.

Shifting Consciousness

In order to summon, charge, and release the magical energy, it is usually necessary for the mind to be in an altered state of consciousness; usually a light trance state of alpha brainwave activity. This is easily accomplished through virtually any form of meditation or even by closing your eyes for a few minutes while concentrating on your goal. After this, you can proceed with the rest of the working.

Projection

It is important to remember that magic involves the movement of energy. It is not just visualization or affirmation, though those techniques usually have their roles to play in the overall process. The single thing that separates magic from positive thinking, daydreaming, or wishing is the conscious, deliberate movement of energy, so it is vital to the work to remember to project the power toward the goal. Mentally send it out to the goal (or the focus such as a candle, herb, or charm) using visualization, feeling, and sheer force of will. Release the energy and it will begin to effect change.

Now that the basics have been covered, we can delve into the good stuff; the actual magic. Since the calendar year begins on January 1, the place to start our journey is that powerful season of winter.

SECTION 1

....

WINTER WONDERLAND

As the earth in her orbit leans us away from the direct rays of the sun, the days grow colder, the weather shifts deeper into clouds and icy winds, and the influence of the power of night reaches its zenith. The nature of winter is dual; physically that of rest, the needed repose which provides the strength and foundation for the coming cycle of growth, but underneath this surface lays a deeper force. Winter, the actual solstice in particular, carries within itself the power of birth. If so inclined, we can harness the prevailing energies of this season in order to cultivate a solid base from which to build our momentum into the new year. We can also nurture that to which we are deeply connected: family, pets, friends, home, et cetera, so that all is sustained through the potentially harsh environment this season can bring.

CHAPTER 2

Power of Winter

The focus of winter in nature is primarily to rest. The leaves have fallen from the trees and the crops have already given up their bounty. With the multitude of colorful blossoms long since scattered to the winds and the once vibrant green stalks, vines, and stems of the plants that produce much of our food left withered and decayed, the life energies of the plant kingdom tend to concentrate in the root systems. Winter also signals the time of rest for much of the animal world. Many insects have a winter dormancy or if their life cycle is short, their eggs may be dormant in winter to hatch in the spring. Larger animals such as some bats, snakes, skunks, chipmunks, and of course bears go into a hibernation cycle for a variety of reasons and this helps them to endure the barren season. Up until relatively recently, the focus of human society during winter was primarily to rest as well. After all of the crops were harvested and the weather turned cold, dark, and foreboding, most people would tend to stay in their own regions and avoid long-distance travel in deference to the potentially hazardous conditions.

Nowadays, much of our society does not have the ability (and/or the desire) to live in harmony with the natural seasonal cycles of life. We are usually expected to follow the modern concept of time such as adhering to the "work week," the school calendar, and appointment schedules which never seem to allow for extended periods of rest, harsh weather patterns, or unapproved holidays. It is most often assumed that we will treat all weekdays as "typical weekdays" regardless of whether the sun is blazing in a hot August sky or winter's icy grip has captured the town, plunging the temperature below freezing. In modern times, it *is* usually necessary to do so, which can have the unfortunate consequence of keeping ourselves so focused on the day-to-day that we can become disconnected from the greater whole.

As magical people, we can strive to develop that special connection to the natural cycles of the earth. One of the ways that we do this is through the acknowledgement of the seasonal shifts and holidays such as the winter solstice and Imbolc. In doing so, we become reacquainted with the ebb and flow of the inherent energies within the land as they connect with our own and discover (or reinforce) how that merging can be used to enrich our lives.

Blessings of the Season

Despite the fact the winter is considered a time of scarcity, there are still some vegetables that can be grown during this time if the weather is not too icy. Winter squashes, sweet potatoes, turnips, kale, Brussels sprouts, and so on can be grown into the winter if they are protected from frost. In fact, turnips develop a somewhat sweeter flavor if they are exposed to a mild frost before they are harvested. Whether or not we choose to have a winter garden, all the vegetables we would need are available at the supermarket. We are now in the time of the "global marketplace" where fresh vegetables and fruits can be imported from the other side of the world to always keep a continuous supply at our fingertips. Even so, it does benefit us to at least attempt to eat seasonally, if not locally, in order to keep our focus in tune with our environment.

Though most of the items offered at the supermarket are intended as food, we need not limit our use of the herbs, vegetables, and fruits solely to cooking. The magical power of what have come to be considered everyday ingredients can in fact be quite profound. A prime example of this is found in the humble turnip.

Roots of Protection

The turnip is a root vegetable that has powerful protective and banishing qualities. It can be used in foods for these purposes, stored in the home, or as in this spell; it can be grown so that it increases in strength and protective power throughout the dark time of the year.

Turnip tops (protection)

Water in a glass

Soil

Flowerpot

Hold the turnip tops in both hands and charge them with protective energy. Plant them in the soil in the flowerpot so that the green tips are sticking through the dirt and the bit of turnip is buried underneath (they root fairly easily; similar to potatoes without the eyes). Cleanse the water of any incorrect energies and water the flowerpot with it as you say the spell to seal the intent.

> *Power of earth and ruled by the moon,*
> *Turnips take root and protect this space.*
> *Charged with power; mystical boon,*
> *Day by day increase in strength.*
> *Guardian plant; blessed with growth,*
> *Shield from harm and nurture our home.*
> *For good of all and by free will,*
> *Magical promise, now fulfill.*

Place the flowerpot either outside or in a sunny window and tend the plant well as it grows. As the plant develops, it will radiate a protective aura essentially acting as a living amulet and ally. Once the turnips are ready to be harvested, they can be eaten to bring protective energy within as well.

Aside from the need for protection during the dark time of the year, there can also be a need for energy. Between the changes in weather and the shortened hours of sunlight, many people tend to feel run down and in need of a boost. Other than increasing the intake of that wonderful elixir known as caffeine, an actual potion for increased energy can be helpful (and healthier).

Energy Potion

1 apple (magic)

1 teaspoon rosemary (all-purpose)

1 peppermint tea bag (energy, purification)

1 teaspoon sage (energy, cleansing)

Pinch ginger (power)

2 cups water

Core and chop the apple, taking care to remove all the seeds. Place it in a cauldron or pot along with the water and herbs. Simmer the liquid on low heat for about 10 to 15 minutes until it is just about to boil. Remove from heat, cover, and allow it to cool to the desired level. Strain the potion into a cup and charge it with the intent that it help to clear your mind and lend you energy and vitality; fill it with pure white light. This potion can be sweetened with honey or pure maple syrup if desired, but I think it is fine on its own. It tastes similar to mulled cider. If you like the taste, you can use the herb/apple remains for an applesauce.

Now if on the other hand you would rather just have a cup of coffee for an energy boost, there is simple way to help speed up its vitalizing effects.

The Coffee Meditation

1 cup coffee, prepared according to taste
  (energy, clarity)

After you've made the cup of coffee, find a comfortable place to sit and take slow sips from the cup. Close your eyes (or at least relax them) and as you sip the coffee, feel the warmth of it as if it is being immediately absorbed into your whole body; awakening every cell while at the same time, soothing away stress and discomfort. Visualize golden, sparkly energy being released from each sip of coffee into your system. Once the cup is empty, open your eyes, stretch, and stand up again to end the meditation.

The winter season brings a few unusual treasures into the supermarkets that are not there the rest of the year. Items such as wreaths and trees (frequently pine or fir), pinecones (often artificially scented however), and fresh cranberries. While the evergreens are not supermarket items in the strictest sense, they are available at this time and are usually a part of traditional winter decorating. It is a longstanding practice to bring greenery indoors during winter to add vitality and a renewed atmosphere into the home. It is a good idea to decorate from the front door (perhaps with a wreath on the door itself), through the home and finish at the back so that the life energy is fully invited indoors. However you may choose to decorate for the season: wreaths, evergreen garlands, bowls of ornamental pinecones or potpourris, and/or a Yule/Christmas tree, any or all of the decorations can be charged with the intention that they release their energies into the home. In general, the properties of the most prominent evergreens for sale—spruce, fir, and pine—are protective, purifying, strengthening, healing and vitalizing, so calling upon their power to fill your home has an uplifting effect on the atmosphere. To charge the evergreens, it is a good idea to bless them and give respect to the spirit of the trees from which they were taken.

Decoration Consecration

Item to be consecrated (tree, garland, wreath, etc.)

Pure water in a cup

Hold the cup of water in both hands and visualize white light pouring into it from your hands and say, "I cleanse this water and cast out any incorrect energies, replacing them with gratitude and blessing." Touch the decoration with your hand and connect with its energy. Mentally thank the essence of the tree (or bush, plant) that was its original form for its sacrifice and ask that it serve your purpose of purifying and vitalizing your home. Let go of the decoration and use the same hand to sprinkle some of the water from the cup on it while saying,

> *Green earth spirit; lend your power to our home,*
> *help us keep safe and free from quarrel,*
> *cleanse the air with your aura,*
> *bless our space with your charm.*
> *Magic of root, vine, plant, and tree,*
> *for good of all, so mote it be.*

Arrange the decoration to your liking. If it is a Christmas/ Yule tree (or potted plant), the remaining water in the cup can be used to water it.

Simmering Potpourris

One of the strongest mental and emotional triggers we have is the power of scent. The smell of chocolate chip cookies baking in the oven, the warm, smoky aroma of a crackling fire, the crisp biting fragrance of a Douglas fir tree decorated in the living room and warmed by colorful lights; these can all evoke wonderful memories and powerful emotion. Aside from their value in this regard, the scent and energy of specific herbal mixtures can be used to create a magical effect. This is of course one of the primary reasons for using incense in spellwork but we can also use a simmering potpourri with similar (and less magically conspicuous) results.

SIMMERING WINTER POTPOURRI

This recipe will fill your home with a wonderful wintertime aroma; it will also imbue the atmosphere with protective, loving, healing, and spiritual vibrations which are an ideal influence during this time of year.

½ cup cranberry sauce (love, protection)

2 tablespoons rosemary (purification,
    protection, love)

1 orange, sliced (love)

2 tablespoons pumpkin pie spice
    (love, spirituality, healing)

1 cup water

Charge each of the ingredients and then combine them in a pot. I use a 2-quart size pot and this mixture fills it about halfway. I don't recommend using a cauldron for this potpourri since as it simmers it will condense down into a thicker, sticky consistency which would be difficult to clean from cast iron without having to re-season it. If you prefer, you could use fresh cranberries instead of canned cranberry sauce to cut down on the thick consistency, but the canned sauce is less expensive and easier to find. Also if a slow cooker is used, adding a liner would make the cleanup a lot easier. If set on low, this blend can simmer for at least a couple of hours, just be sure to check on it, and stirring every so often can help to release more fragrance.

Fruit of Winter

Though mostly thought of as a summertime staple, before modern variety creation, cultivation, and importation, oranges were primarily available during winter. These fruits provided a welcome change of pace and dose of vitamin C. In the magical arena, the orange is a valuable ingredient in spells and recipes designed for love, beauty, luck, and prosperity. Oranges are very multifunctional, the juice can be used a substitute for wine (as can cranberry or grape juice) and they can become charms for a variety of purposes depending upon what is added to them. A good example of this is in the use of an orange to create a pomander charm. Originally, a pomander was a vessel designed to hold herbs and fragrant spices in order to ward off illness, insects or danger.[1] The pomander then evolved from being a container in which herbs are stored for medicinal or magical purposes to being only an ornamental object to provide fragrance. This is coming full circle in modern times with a renewed interest in the magical potential of such an unusual item.

All-Purpose Pomander Charm

1 orange (love, luck, money)

1 pack straight pins (multicolored if possible)

1 ribbon in corresponding color (see color chart on page 305)

---

1   Robert Chambers, *The Book of Days* (W & R Chambers, 1864), 291.

Whole cloves (protection, love, money)

Wooden skewer (or toothpick or nail)

Symbol of intent (scroll, charm, etc.)

Cover a work space with a towel to catch the juice that will inevitably fall from the orange. Prepare a design that symbolizes the intent of this working. This symbol can be as simple as a small scroll of paper with your intent written on it, a metal charm with a talisman engraved upon it, a piece of material with a symbol sewn, embroidered, or painted on it; there are many options. The only rule of thumb regarding the symbol should be that it can be somehow affixed to the completed pomander. In the case of a scroll or metal charm, they can be tied to the ribbon during the creation process.

To create the pomander, tie the ribbon around the orange: crisscross it on the bottom, and tie it at the top like wrapping a present. Use the pins to hold the ribbon in place. Now, using the ribbon lines as reference points, poke holes in the orange as evenly as you can with the skewer and then place a whole clove into each guide-hole as securely as possible. When the orange is as covered in cloves as desired, focus strongly upon your goal and tie three knots in the top of the ribbon to bind your intent. It is at this point you can add a scroll or metal charm, tying it into the first of the three knots. Next, hold the pomander in both hands, again focusing on the goal and say:

> *Winter's fruit, lending energy that is yours, adorned with pins and magical spice; sealed with power and knotted thrice , vessel of [state intention], release the force.*

Hang the pomander in a cool, dark place for about a week so that it can dry out a bit and then it can be openly displayed if desired.

The season of winter, though a somewhat vulnerable time can also be a magical span of beauty, joy, and reverence. Temperatures may drop, rain and snow may fall (sometimes in a seemingly endless volume), and the dark may appear to have an excessive amount of dominance, but throughout this time a delicate interplay of forces occurs holding within its dance a promise of greater things.

Winter Shopping List
- Apple
- Cloves (whole)
- Coffee
- Cranberry sauce
- Decoration of choice
- Ginger
- Mint (or mint tea bags)
- Orange
- Pumpkin pie spice

- Ribbon
- Rosemary
- Sage
- Straight pins (multicolored if possible)
- Wooden skewer (or toothpick or nail)

CHAPTER 3

Solstice of Earth and Air

Given the fact that the seasons of the planet are divided based on which hemisphere is angled toward the sun to a greater degree at the time, the energy contained in the seasons can be experienced differently depending on which hemisphere a person is located.

Northern Hemisphere: The exact moment of the winter solstice occurs when the earth is positioned so that the sun is over the tropic of Capricorn, the southernmost line of latitude where the sun can be directly overhead. At this same time, the sun moves into the astrological sign of Capricorn, the cardinal (initiatory) zodiac sign of the winter solstice. This sign is of the earth element, and the season of winter is often thought to be aligned with the element of earth as this is the time of earth's slumber. As the season progresses in the Northern Hemisphere, the sun moves through Capricorn and into the "fixed" sign of Aquarius, an air sign. The fixed signs of the zodiac—Taurus, Leo, Scorpio, and Aquarius—are the ones that exemplify their season and arrive when their given span is fully established. With this understanding, it becomes apparent that wintertime in the north is not only aligned to the element of earth but also to the element of air. The way I view this is that winter showcases the power of earth in its passive aspect and the power of air in its active aspect. Essentially, my perspective on this dynamic is that the grounding, introspective, meditative focus of the earth element is most effectively channeled at this time as is the creative, expressionist, communicative power of air.

Southern Hemisphere: The opposite weather is experienced in the southern part of the globe, when the north is entering summer, the south is beginning their winter. In the Southern Hemisphere, winter begins as the sun reaches the Tropic of Cancer, the northernmost line of latitude at which the sun will shine directly overhead and (unsurprisingly), enters the zodiac sign of Cancer as well. This is the cardinal (initiatory) sign of the water element. As the season progresses, it moves into the fixed sign of Leo; a fire sign, which illustrates a very different type of winter season than that experienced in the north. This water/fire style winter, though cold, does not share many of the features of winter in the Northern Hemisphere. Looking at a globe, it is clear to see that there is considerably more land mass in the Northern Hemisphere and a much larger area of water in the south. Naturally, this gives water a more dominant presence.

Additionally, the Northern Hemisphere land masses tend to have larger areas of higher elevation than do the land masses of the south; the two main exceptions being the Andes and the New Zealand Alps. Since snow under normal circumstances needs both moisture and high elevation to develop, snow is rare in most areas of the Southern Hemisphere (excluding Antarctica of course). This is a primary reason why for example, the Winter Olympic games are held almost entirely in nations in the Northern Hemisphere. It's not that winter is colder or stronger in the north, it is merely more likely to be snowy and icy; necessary qualities for most winter events. Regardless of hemisphere, winter signifies the same thing; rest, repose, renewal, and in the time of darkness, that rebirth of light, the glimmer of hope that is the child of promise.

The Child of Promise

Within the seemingly all-encompassing shroud of darkness that appears to fall about the world when we reach the time of winter, a single, precious gleam of light is born and begins to grow; this is the child of promise. Much has been written about the concept of this child. Some see this as a metaphor for our own individual reemergence from the confines of the dark half of the year, into a new cycle of vibrancy and creativity. Others link the child of promise directly to myth and see the child as an expression of one of the deities born at this time such as Saturn, Mithra, Dionysus, Horus, Attis, Amaterasu, and Lucina, or gods associated with youth or transformation such as Hebe or Mabon. Some are more literal and see the child as simply a metaphor for the sun itself, whose annual cycle of lengthening and shortening of days restarts on the solstice.

Personally, I think each of these viewpoints has merit and feel that this time of the year can be used to revitalize our inner selves, honor the reborn divinity, and acknowledge the return of the waxing solar cycle; nothing need be overlooked or excluded. To connect to the child of promise within and unleash the dormant creative power that this attunement can bring, the following ritual can be of assistance.

Strengthening the Inner Child of Promise

This is a three-part process; a ritual of acknowledgement and reconnection. The first part is the creation of the ritual beverage. This drink has the qualities of love, healing, cleansing, protection, and prosperity which are ideal for nurturing your inner child. Who knew that the humble mug of hot cocoa contained so much untapped energy?

Magical Old-Fashioned Hot Cocoa

3 tablespoons unsweetened cocoa powder
(prosperity and love)

¼ cup sugar (love, cleansing) or stevia sweetener
(healing, success)

2¼ cups milk (healing, protection)

¼ teaspoon vanilla extract (love, energy)

In a small pot, combine the sugar and cocoa powder, whisking lightly to blend. Slowly whisk in ¼ cup of milk so that a chocolatey paste is formed. Heat on medium and add another ¼ cup of milk, stirring constantly until milk just begins to boil. Add the remaining milk and stir. Remove from heat and add the vanilla. Charge it with the energy of love and comfort. Pour the desired amount into a mug and sip it while preparing for the following exercise.

Greeting the Inner Child of Promise

A simple meditation can be used to awaken your awareness of the inner child. Find a comfortable place to sit and close your eyes. Think back on a pleasant memory from childhood. Remember a time when you were playing and felt carefree. Try to move from an analytical mindset and focus on how you felt while playing; remember. Reminisce and mentally relive that frame of mind. As children we aren't as burdened by our rational sides so our scope of imagination is limitless. Invoke within yourself that feeling of limitless possibility. Greet who you once were, and realize this child is still within you and is a blessing. Invite them to be a greater influence in your life and promise that you will take time out to respect their needs instead of solely focusing on adult matters. When you feel properly connected, thank them for their help and vow to spend time with them again. Say farewell and end the meditation.

Unleashing the Inner Child of Promise

For this part of the process, a few items will be needed. Crayons, colored pencils, or watercolor paints, and a coloring book. If some of the cocoa is available, sipping it during this exercise is helpful. Try to use a coloring book that is either nostalgic or magical in nature. Coloring books of some fashion can usually be found in most of the larger supermarkets today, as can crayons in the office supply/ stationery or book/magazine section. Books with coloring pages of mandalas or other intricate designs can be excellent for this, as can the *Witch's Coloring Book* (Llewellyn, 2016), but whatever you can find will do. Once the book is chosen, sit down in a comfortable place, relax, and begin to color in a picture. Don't try to plan or overanalyze how you want the finished product to look; that is the left-brained thinking trying to force its influence. Instead, allow your spontaneous inner creativity to blossom. Let the inner child have their moment. When you are finished with the picture, you can cut it out of the book and either frame it as a keepsake or even put it up on the refrigerator as an affirmation that you are pleased with the work of your inner child and that you wish to continue to draw upon their influence and ability. As an alternative, you could leave the page in the coloring book and work this exercise again on a regular basis, perhaps once a week, and color a different page each time until the book is full.

Though many recipes for magical inks exist (some of which are quite ancient), a modern and very inner child-friendly method of creating a magical pigment is the making of our own watercolor paints. These paints can be used to create a magically charged picture that radiates our magical intent. You can use them exactly as you would those trays of dried watercolor paints; dip your brush in water and then swirl in the color until it is rehydrated, then paint whatever rune, symbol, or picture suits your magical goal.

MAGICAL WATERCOLOR PAINT

These paints are enhanced with a small amount of a powdered herb to contribute magical energy and fragrance. The herb chosen is dependent upon the goal in mind. The only rule of thumb is to make sure that the herb is available in a finely powdered form.

4 tablespoons baking soda

2 tablespoons white vinegar

2 tablespoons cornstarch

1 tablespoon water (or more if needed)

½ teaspoon corn syrup

¼ teaspoon powdered herb (see correspondence
   table on page 307 for ideas)

Food coloring (in chosen color)

Stir baking soda and vinegar together until they stop fizz-
ing. Add the cornstarch and water and mix together until
smooth. Add the powdered herb and corn syrup and stir
again until smooth. Add several drops of the food coloring
until the desired shade is achieved. Pour into a container
and charge the paint with your magical goal. Allow the
paint to set and dry overnight before use.

Using things like crayons and paints can help to restore
that connection to our inner child and this can be a wonderful enhancement to our magical practice (through greater
access to our imaginative side) and our everyday lives. This
personal view of the child of promise is but one aspect of
this important concept. To honor the divine child can be
one of the major themes of the holiday celebration of Yule.

HOLIDAY: Yuletide

The name *Yule* has in modern times become the almost universal name for the winter solstice holiday. As noted, the winter solstice is not only the time of the least amount of light; the shortest day and longest night, but also the new beginning, the re-birth of the sun. Practically speaking, this holiday is at a time that is usually cold with difficult weather conditions and sometimes food is scarce. Even today with the access to modern supermarkets, food stocks can run short in prolonged periods of bad weather or for a host of other reasons. On each of the holidays, but perhaps most poignantly with the winter festivals, it is traditional to gather together in celebration and feasting.

Creating a large feast is a wonderful way to celebrate the holiday and reaffirm a commitment to abundance and joyous living, despite the dormant, cold time of year. This feast needn't be a burden on one, but can instead be a potluck-style group effort with traditional foods such as home baked breads and sweets, vegetables, stews, ciders and more each made by a different person. In addition to food, there are of course wonderful decorations, gifts, and many more ways to create a delightful holiday atmosphere. The simmering potpourri described in chapter 2 can be used to lend ambience, as can the following recipes.

Simmering Potpourris

One of the key aspects of winter in most folklore is that the short days and long nights can leave one vulnerable to danger. Thus, protection magic is a valuable option to help lessen any possibility of mishap or trouble. When brewed, this potpourri releases protective energies into the home, creating a more safeguarded environment.

Simmering Protection Potpourri

¼ cup bay leaves (purification)

4 or 5 peppermint tea bags (purification)

¼ cup rosemary (purification, protection)

Sprig of fir, optional (blessing, protection)

2 cups water

Crumble the dry ingredients and charge them with protective intent. Add them to a pot along with the water. Simmer on low heat to allow the fragrance and energy to be released, being sure to add water as needed so it doesn't run out.

Brews

In this book, each of the holidays listed will have a brew associated with it that will help you to connect with the energies present at that time of the year. These types of brews are generally known as attunement teas. One of my favorite recipes to use for the Yuletide tea is the following.

Yuletide Attunement Tea

1 tablespoon cranberry juice (protection)

1 peppermint tea bag (healing, purification)

1 regular "black tea" tea bag (courage)

2 cups water

Heat the water in a pot just below the boiling point when little bubbles appear at the bottom of the pot. Remove from heat and add the tea. Steep both tea bags in the water and once the tea is ready, add the cranberry juice and any sweetener if desired. Charge the tea with the feeling of winter. Sip to attune to the energy of the season.

Incense

The delightfully woodsy and spicy scent of the smoke of this incense lends an appropriately enchanting atmosphere to the Yule ritual or at any other time during the season.

Yuletide Spice Incense

1 tablespoon pine, spruce, fir, or a sprig off
   the tree (for protection)

1 tablespoon rosemary (remembrance,
   protection, love)

1 teaspoon cinnamon (love and spirituality)

1 teaspoon grated and dried orange peel
   (love, luck)

¼ teaspoon pumpkin pie spice (love,
   luck, healing)

Make sure that the ingredients are completely dried and either grind down the rosemary and evergreen sprigs or snip them into little pieces with a sturdy pair of kitchen shears. If you don't have a live tree, wreath, or garland, you can substitute an additional tablespoon of rosemary since this is a similarly scented and multipurpose herb. Combine all ingredients in a bowl and charge with the intent that this mixture will be filled with and help connect to the energies of the season (basically, fill yourself with the Yuletide spirit and project it into the incense mixture). Transfer the incense into a container with a tight-fitting lid and use as desired.

Oils

These handy sabbat oils can be used for ritual anointing purposes, as a homemade gift idea for witchy loved ones, and as a magical oil in spells for love, luck, or protection.

YULE'S FIRE OIL

1 tablespoon rosemary (remembrance, protection, love)

¼ teaspoon cinnamon (love, spirituality)

¼ teaspoon orange zest (love, luck)

½ cup sunflower oil (solar energy, luck)

Each of these ingredients offers energy related to the sun which is perfectly attuned to this time of the sun's rebirth.

If sunflower oil is difficult to find or prohibitively expensive (it seems to be getting increasingly rare, at least in my area), corn oil can be used as a reasonable substitute in this or any of the other recipes calling for sunflower oil. If the oil needs to be substituted, but you still wish to draw in the energy of the sunflower, add a teaspoon of ground sunflower seeds to the recipe. This preserves the energetic balance of the oil while still keeping things simple to prepare.

Prepare the oil according to the standard directions for creating a magical oil (given on page 7). Charge with the energy of the season in a similar manner as you did for the Yule incense previously, then strain and bottle.

Oil Spells

This spell is used to create a classic decorative garland that is also a powerful amulet of protection for the home. This amulet is designed not as a shield, but rather as a magical filter to inhibit, neutralize, and banish harm and for that reason and also because we are entering the time of the winter solstice, we shall be calling upon the energy of Saturn (the planetary ruler of Capricorn). To lend the Saturn energy, take the already prepared Yule oil, place in a pot and add 1 tablespoon grated beet. Simmer on low heat for 2 to 5 minutes, strain, cool, and recharge the oil, calling upon the power of Saturn to neutralize and ground all energies or forces that may come to do harm. Rebottle the Saturn/Yule oil.

Garland of Protection

Sturdy tapestry needle

Heavy-duty sewing thread or waxed dental floss

Prepared popcorn (protection)

Fresh cranberries (protection)

1 bottle Saturn/Yule oil

Allow the popped popcorn (air-popped works best) to sit out for at least one day to turn a bit stale, as this makes it much easier to string; freshly popped corn kernels tend to break. The cranberries however can be fresh. Since cranberries can be juicy, it is a very good idea to use a drop cloth or cover the working area with lots of newspaper. If you have a lot of plastic bags from the supermarket, using them to cover the working area is a nice way to get a second use out of them. It's also a good idea to wear old clothes or an apron or smock to avoid stains. After you have gathered all of your ingredients and supplies, measure out the desired length of thread adding an additional 2 feet to however long you want the finished garland to be; doubling the thread for strength if needed. Thread the needle and tie a thick double or triple knot at the end, leaving about a foot of the cord hanging past the knot.

Now cover the thread with some of the Saturn/Yule Oil, wetting your fingers with the oil and sliding them over the length of the thread to coat. This will catalyze your intent into the finished garland. Popcorn and cranberries both have naturally protective qualities and the addition of the oil brings everything together into a single purpose. Next, begin to string the cranberries and popcorn kernels in whatever pattern is most pleasing to you. You can work using number magic. Various numbers have been attributed to Saturn; most notably 3 (and its multiples 6 and 9) and the number 7. You could work with any of these numbers, stringing the popcorn and cranberries in alternate number combinations, or the number 8 can be used for the number of the sabbats, or an informal random pattern can be utilized.

When you have finished stringing the "beads" of corn and cranberry, tie a knot in end of the cord, again leaving about a foot of length after the knot and snip it so that the needle is freed. Finally, coil the garland so that you can place both hands over it and charge it with your intent using this (or a similar) spell to seal the charge.

By free will, for highest good,
this spell is fixed with sacred food;
fruit and seed, together entwined,
with Saturn's energy to bind the charm;
garland of magic does now combine,
strength and power to protect this home.

The garland can now be hung as a decoration either indoors or out. Several of these can be made and draped over bushes outside which would not only serve as a protection for your home, but also would provide some winter food for whatever birds might be in the neighborhood.

Powders

The ingredients of this magical powder combine to offer the energies of protection, love, and peace which are perfect for creating the proper atmosphere for the holiday season. Purchasing most of the dry items pre-ground would make preparation much easier, and quite a lot of this powder can be made and used in a variety of ways.

SOLSTICE DUST

1 tablespoon cinnamon (love, spirituality)

1 tablespoon cloves (protection)

1 tablespoon nutmeg (love)

1 tablespoon sage (protection)

Chamomile, 1 tea bag (peace)

2 drops vanilla extract (peace)

2 drops orange extract (love)

Cornstarch (optional)

Combine the first five ingredients in a bowl and powder them together with your fingers, a spoon, or use a mortar and pestle. Once the herbs have been finely powdered, add the vanilla and orange extracts. Stir to blend and if the mixture is too moist, add some cornstarch just until the powder feels dry. Leave out to dry overnight then charge with intent (for love, peace, and protection) and bottle for use.

POWDER SPELLS

This spell charges the energy of a room with a delightful vibe which can help maintain a pleasant feeling when hosting a large gathering of friends and family. If you are setting up a dinner party for the holiday, you can create these in large amounts to be used as strategically placed decorations or tree ornaments to keep a calm atmosphere attuned to the season.

Mini Witch Balls

1 box white household candles

Small pot or double boiler

Cupcake pan

Aluminum foil

Decorative ribbon, twist ties, or ornament hooks

Solstice dust

Yule's Fire oil

Melon baller or 1-teaspoon-sized measuring
    spoon (optional)

Line the cupcake pan with a sheet of foil. My preferred methods are either to use a single large sheet of foil and press it down into each cup so that the whole pan is covered and safe from unwanted wax drippings, or to cut squares of foil, one per cup, leaving enough overhang to protect the pan. Grease each cup with a little dab of Yule's Fire oil. This will not only lend energy but also allow the finished product to release free from the pan. If the magical oil is not available, it is fine to simply spray the cups with a little cooking spray or regular oil to grease them.

Once the pan has been prepared, break up the candles into the pot or double boiler and melt the wax on the stove slowly over very low heat. Once the wax is fully melted, swirl in a tablespoon or two of the Solstice dust and remove from heat. Carefully pour the melted wax into the cupcake cups, being sure not to overfill or spill the wax. After the cups are filled, allow the wax mixture to cool somewhat before the next step (approximately 25 minutes) so that it is no longer liquid but still soft.

There are two possible methods for forming the balls. Method 1: Grease the melon baller and use it to carefully scoop out small wax balls from the cupcake cups, setting them on a cookie sheet to finish cooling; when they have hardened, they can be wrapped in foil, twisting the foil at the top (so that they resemble little candies), wrapping an ornament hook around the twist to secure it. Method 2: Using the individual foil squares in the pan when the wax has semi-cooled, pull up the corners of the foil, molding the wax into a ball, being careful to avoid squishing any wax up through the opening at the top. Twist the foil around the ball of wax, adding an ornament wire to secure it. This second method creates a larger sized ball about the size of an apricot. Using either method once the balls have been made, they can be further embellished with curly gift ribbons and hung on the tree or tucked into other decorations such as mantle garlands or wreaths.

Charms

Most of the magic traditionally associated with the sabbats of the dark half of the year relates to protection. There are many practical reasons for this even in modern times such as weather, darkness, and increased holiday traffic, to name but a few. With a little magic peppered throughout our Yuletide, we can rest assured that the holiday will run as smoothly as possible. The following magical charm is cleverly disguised as an adorable decoration. These ornaments mimic gingerbread cookies though their ingredients are charged to become a powerful protective force.

Magical "Cookie" Ornaments

1¾ cup flour

3 tablespoons plus 1 teaspoon cinnamon, powdered (protection)

1 teaspoon ginger, powdered (protection)

1 teaspoon cloves, powdered (protection, banishing)

1⅓ cup water

1 cup salt

⅓ cup cornstarch

Mix the salt into 1 cup of water. Heat the saltwater until just about to boil. Meanwhile, sift the cinnamon and flour together. Dissolve the cornstarch into ⅓ cup of water. Add the ginger and cloves, and combine the cornstarch mixture with the saltwater. Stir in the cinnamon flour to make dough. Roll out the dough to ¼-inch thickness. Using one large or a series of smaller cookie cutters, create the desired shapes in the dough and remove to a baking sheet. Using a drinking straw or skewer, carefully pierce each ornament once to create a hole for hanging. Bake at 350° Fahrenheit for 30 minutes to properly dry out the ornaments. Take them out of the oven and allow to cool before removing them from the pan. Once completely cooled, thread a ribbon through the hole to create a loop for hanging the ornament, and charge with intent for protection.

This next charm is also disguised as a lovely holiday decoration. It draws upon the magic of what is considered by some Witches to be a sacred fruit—the apple.

Apple Swag

Apples, sliced ⅛-inch thick (faery magic,
 healing, love)

Raffia ribbon

Lemon juice

The amount of apples and raffia needed will vary based on how long you want the swag to be. Slice as many apples as desired. Soak apples for 30 minutes in lemon juice so the apples don't turn brown. Lay the apples in a single layer on a parchment paper-lined cookie sheet, and place in a warm oven (or food dehydrator) until completely dry. In a 200° F oven, the apples will take approximately 2 to 3 hours and should be flipped once an hour for even crispness. In a food dehydrator set at 135° F, they will take between 6 to 8 hours to dry completely. Once dried, charge the apples with the energy of love and/or healing so they will radiate a positive influence in your home. They can now be strung together on the raffia ribbon or another natural cord and hung as a garland on a Yule tree, a mantle, or wound through a wreath.

The dried apple slices can also be layered with peanut butter and birdseed and strung on a raffia loop (or sturdy floral wire) to make a decorative and magical winter bird feeder to hang on an outdoor tree branch or hook. The apples can be left out for wildlife after the holiday, though make sure no seeds are still attached, the raffia is removed, and the slices are broken into smaller pieces so they are easier to eat. The individual slices of apple could also be tied separately with the raffia or shiny ribbon to be hung on a Yule tree as surprisingly attractive magical ornaments as can other fruits such as the previously mentioned "fruit of winter," the orange. Oranges can be tied up with colorful ribbons and added to the Yule tree as natural bulbs as can the pomander charm from chapter 2. Those can be charged for protection and added to the tree in order protect the gifts placed beneath it from theft or harm.

Foods

The foods of Yule are relatively standard winter holiday fare: turkey, mashed potatoes, cakes, cookies, homemade fruit breads, and many other treats. Any "regular" recipe can be transformed into a magical dish; all that is needed is knowledge of the magical correspondences or the ingredients used in the recipe. Using the ingredients correspondence list at the back of this book, look up the main ingredients in whichever recipe you want to transform, and write down their magical attributes. Once you have the list of magical uses, you can then decide which of these qualities you would like to charge the complete dish to manifest.

As an example, the following traditional holiday cider has many ingredients to consider and can be used magically for a couple of different purposes. As you can see on the following annotated list, love magic, protection, purification/cleansing, lunar, and faery magic are all possibilities. It is best to bring out whatever is the most dominant natural qualities already present amongst the ingredients, so using the cider for hex breaking (an attribute of the optional star anise) would not be the best option, as it is indicated in only one ingredient. There are six edible ingredients in this recipe with the primary ingredient being apple cider or juice. The lemon peel, cinnamon, cloves, and juice are all attuned to love. This seems to be the best choice and will help keep everyone in a loving holiday mood.

Yuletide Mulled Cider

2 twelve-inch cheesecloth squares

1 ten-inch piece of kitchen twine or
cotton thread

8 strips lemon peel (purification, love,
moon magic)

8 cinnamon sticks (spirituality, love, success)

8 whole star anise pods (*optional*; psychic
ability, protection, hex breaking)

2 teaspoons whole cloves (banishing, protection,
love, money)

2 teaspoons whole allspice (money, luck, healing)

1½ gallons apple cider or juice (love, healing,
faery magic)

Place the layers of cheesecloth on top of each other creating a single square. Combine all the herbs and spices into the center of the cheesecloth and gather up the corners, trapping the ingredients inside, and tie with the kitchen twine or thread, creating a sachet. Star anise can be difficult to find. In some areas they can only be found at specialty Asian markets or health food stores, which is why their inclusion is optional. Once prepared, hold the sachet in both hands and charge with the energy of the season. Fill a pot with the apple cider and add the sachet. Bring to a boil, then reduce heat to medium and simmer for 10 minutes. Serve.

Bowl of Magical Wisdom

Magic is everywhere; it permeates everything from the most ethereal and cosmic to the most basic and mundane—and this is the secret of kitchen witchery. Even a simple bowl of snacks can be a reservoir of magical energy that can nourish our spirits as well as our bodies. In this case, magically empowering some whole mixed nuts can help them become a powerful aid to wisdom, inspiration, and clear, more focused thinking.

1 bowl (ideally, earthenware with 3 cup-capacity)

1 cup almonds, whole (wisdom)

1 cup walnuts, whole (wisdom)

1 cup filberts (hazelnuts), whole (wisdom)

Charge each cup of nuts individually for wisdom and combine together in the bowl, mixing them together with your hands to distribute them evenly and to mingle their energies. Place the bowl in an easily accessible area with a nutcracker and an empty bowl to hold the shells. Do so with the intent that "all who eat of these nuts shall gain wisdom, only according to free will and for the good of all" so as to avoid magical manipulation.

Witch Bottles

In ancient times, witch bottles were primarily focused on protection or curse removal but today we can use magical bottles to contain spells for nearly any purpose. For Yule I like to create a bottle that not only has a magical nature but also doubles as an attractive holiday decoration. This witch bottle can be used to channel and amplify the holiday's energy and can be kept on an altar to enhance any magic for new beginnings, purification, and rebirth.

YULETIDE WITCH BOTTLE

1–2 cups kosher salt

1 piece dried orange peel cut into a circle
(solar energy, love, luck, money)

3 to 5 sprigs fresh rosemary (purification)

Hazelnuts (wisdom)

Wide-mouthed bottle with lid (or canning jar)

Fill the jar halfway with the salt. Slide the orange peel down the edge of the jar pressing it into the salt so that half of the circle is sticking out above the salt. This is meant to resemble the newborn sun rising up out of the snow. Next, stick the rosemary sprigs into the salt so that they resemble trees in a forest. Sprinkle in a few hazelnuts and the snowy winter scene is complete. To charge the bottle, fill yourself with the pleasant "spirit of the season" and send this energy into the bottle. Place the lid on the bottle with the intent that its energy will continue to radiate out as long as it remains sealed. Aside from keeping this bottle on an altar, it could be set out as a decoration on a mantle, coffee table, or countertop.

Ritual

It has never been my intention in any of my writing to reveal or create any new Witchcraft traditions but rather to share magical practices, ideas, and recipes. My focus remains the same, but since this work is centered around the sabbats and seasons, it would make sense to include ritual outlines for these important holidays. What follows will be of the barest framework so that each can be personalized to suit individual needs. With that in mind, these rituals will still only require ingredients from the supermarket to perform and can be woven into other sabbat rituals as desired.

The basic points of interest (so to speak) in regards to the Yule sabbat are frequently: acknowledging rebirth amidst the darkness, greeting the waxing light of the sun, honoring the cosmic mother, connecting to and protecting loved ones, and the theme of the child of promise. Since the inner child of promise aspect of the theme has already been touched upon, it is not addressed again here, but the more divine and stellar facets are.

SOLSTICE TREE OF LIFE RITUAL
Items needed

Yule tree (live or cut, not artificial)

Mini witch ball ornaments (at least one)

Deity decorations, if desired

Water

The basic concept of this working is to use the Yule tree, itself a symbol of connection to the everlasting life force, as a *stang* in order to bridge the gap between realms. A stang is a magical staff that is usually a forked branch from a tree. There are similar properties of both the stang and a tree in magical practice, so the crossover use makes sense. The deity decorations will only be needed if you plan on connecting with deities in ritual; not every Witch does and even those of us that do may not choose to every time. Regardless, if specific deities are being called upon, individual decorations to each one should be created. If the Goddess and God are called upon in less specific forms, decorations can be made in more general terms, e.g., a sun and moon motif.

If these decorations are handmade, almost anything can be used in their creation. Small picture frames can be hung on the tree with wire and small images of the deities can be placed inside. In this digital age images from classical art can be printed out with the click of a mouse. The decorations do not have to be expensive or ostentatious but they should be made from the heart and thoughtful. Once the decorations have been created (or omitted as the case may be) and everything has been assembled near the tree, the work can begin.

If you have the Yule tree in the same room as a ritual altar, so much the better, but if not, the tree itself will essentially acts as an altar so the work can proceed. To begin, cast a circle or perform whatever your standard ritual space preparations are to ready the area. If you choose to call the elements, you can say the following or similar words:

(Turning to the north)

Power of earth, heed my call. Join me in this rite.

This can be repeated in the remaining directions moving clockwise invoking the elements, substituting "power of air" in the east, "power of fire" in the south and "power of water" in the west.[2]

Return to facing north in front of the tree. Touch the branches, mentally connecting with their energy, and feel that the atmosphere is being charged with the elemental forces and that the tree is acting as the focal point and channel for these energies. This can be proclaimed with words such as:

---

2   In the Southern Hemisphere, circles are most often cast "counter-clockwise" because to move in this direction is sunwise there, moving from east to north to west to south.

Through magic rite, here are joined,
Land, Sea, and Sky do merge;
the three great realms of nature combine
With sacred fire to seal the charge.

This draws the energies through the tree and into the center point of the working area.

At this point, the mini witch ball ornaments can be placed on the tree with the intent that the energy of the season shall be peaceful and for the good of all, meaning that we are expressing the intent that the power of winter will be expressed in its most proper form with minimal harm. This is a way of helping to "turn the wheel" by adding your personal energy and intent into the already present forces of the season. Next, add the deity tokens to the tree (if used), one at a time, calling out to each deity as you place the tokens. As an example, if the deities involved are the Great Mother and the new sun/son then as the goddess token is placed, you could say, "Great Mother Goddess, I give thanks to you; the sun is reborn and I rejoice." As the god token is placed, you could say, "Newborn one of the winter sun, grow in strength with each new day."

Once the tokens are in place, touch the tree again and focus on the feeling of connection; not just to the tree and the elements but also to the seasonal shift and to the deities themselves. Open yourself up to the higher spiritual powers. Reach out with your heart and give thanks and joy for the return of the waxing light, the reborn child of promise. As you reach the peak of this feeling of gratitude, you can ask for a blessing of protection for your loved ones using your own words but keeping in mind that it should be done according to their free will (even subconsciously) and for the good of all so as to avoid magical manipulation. After the blessing, offer a gift of water to the tree as a thank-you to all involved. Once this has been done, the rite can be concluded.

To end the rite, thank the deities if you have called them and release the elements.

(Turn to the west):

Power of water, I thank you for attending this rite.

Repeat in each direction substituting "power of fire" in the south, "power of air" in the east, and "power of earth" in the north. Finally, open the circle or conclude the rite in your preferred fashion.

Witchy Ways

Yuletide is one of the busiest holidays of the year for many of us. Considering that there are so many holidays in the month of December and that many of us already have schedules which are quite busy, it can difficult for us to find the time to focus on the spiritual and magical aspects of the season. With luck and good planning, the Yule ceremony can provide that singular moment that allows us to reconnect to that cosmic essence, but it is important to take time out and connect to the energy of the season outside of formal ritual. Since this time of year is so hectic, it can be very difficult to find the free time for quiet connection. Often the only time we have to ourselves is when taking a bath or shower, so we might as well turn that into an opportunity for reflection and connection.

If you are able to really indulge, you can burn the Yule incense and sip the attunement tea while in a bubble bath and relax, letting your mind contemplate the season and its meaning. The light can be dimmed and the winter theme can be enhanced with specialty lighting. A short strand of indoor/outdoor holiday lights can be plugged in and draped over the bathroom mirror to lend a holiday atmosphere. If you are more pressed for time, you could use a holiday-themed nightlight (such as a snowman or snowflake) and a pine-scented candle. In any case, try to have some time—even if for only a few moments—to decompress, reach out, and connect to the spirit of the season. These little connections can be as important in building our practice as regular formal ritual. Despite the hubbub of the holiday season, we can still take time out for reverence and communion, building within ourselves a strong spiritual foundation so that we are ready to step boldly into the new year.

Yuletide Shopping List

- Almonds
- Allspice
- Aluminum foil
- Apple cider
- Apples
- Baking soda
- Bay leaves
- Candles (white, household)
- Chamomile tea bags
- Cheesecloth
- Cinnamon (sticks and powdered)
- Cloves (whole and powdered)
- Cocoa powder (unsweetened)
- Coloring book
- Corn syrup
- Cornstarch
- Cranberry juice
- Cranberries (fresh)
- Crayons, colored pencils, or watercolor paints
- Dental floss or thread

- Filberts (hazelnuts)
- Flour
- Food coloring
- Ginger
- Kitchen twine
- Lemon
- Lemon juice
- Milk
- Nutmeg
- Oranges
- Parchment paper
- Peppermint tea bags
- Pine, spruce, or fir sprigs
- Popcorn
- Pumpkin pie spice
- Raffia ribbon
- Ribbon (or twist ties)
- Rosemary
- Sage
- Salt (kosher and regular)
- Star anise

- Sewing needle
- Sugar or stevia sweetener
- Sunflower oil
- Tea (regular black tea)
- Vanilla extract
- Vinegar (white)
- Walnuts

CHAPTER 4

The New Calendar

A long time ago—the year 45 BCE to be precise—Julius Caesar instituted the Julian calendar and the new year was officially celebrated on January 1. Being that the Julian calendar was slightly out of step with the actual length of the solar year (by roughly eleven minutes per year), adjustments were made at the insistence of Pope Gregory XIII, and in the year 1582 the Gregorian calendar was born. This calendar brought the "wandering" days into alignment so that the year always begins on January 1.

Happy New Year

Celebrating the new year is one of those universal holidays. Every year you can watch television coverage of celebrations all over the world in dozens of different countries and cultures; that so many people focus on a single event and purpose is absolutely magical to me. For the typical modern New Year's Eve celebration, most of us are already used to getting our supplies from the supermarket, so not much adjustment is be needed from the usual champagne, hors d' oeuvres, party hats, and noisemakers.

The underlying theme of the New Year's celebration is renewal; in a fashion similar to Samhain, we can bid farewell to the old year and build hope for the new. As such, a focus of magical work for this time is on cleansing of any unresolved or problematic energy that may linger from the previous year.

Simmering Potpourri

A simple way to charge the atmosphere of the home with a blast of "fresh start" energy is to use this potpourri.

HAPPY NEW YEAR'S POTPOURRI

2 lemons, quartered (purification, love)

1 lime, quartered (purification, healing, love)

1 orange, quartered (love)

1 grapefruit, quartered (purification, healing)

Water

Cut up the citrus fruit and place in a pot with just enough water to cover. Charge the ingredients to provide cleansing and renewal and allow the mixture to simmer on low, adding water as needed, for as long as desired to freshen the atmosphere of the home.

Brews

The classic beverage for a New Year's celebration is of course champagne, which magically relates to abundance, celebration, divine love, and harmony with nature. The bubbles of champagne can be helpful in releasing its energy. To add to the natural properties of champagne, we can prepare a simple mixture that can bolster our wishes and hope for the future in a magically festive fashion.

NEW YEAR'S CHAMPAGNE PUNCH POTION

1 bottle champagne (750 ml) or ginger ale (2 liters)

1 bottle club soda (releasing energy, uniting elements) (2 liters)

2 ounces brandy (optional)

2 ounces triple sec/orange-flavored liqueur (optional)

8 ounces pineapple slices (luck, prosperity)

8 ounces orange slices (luck, prosperity)

1 cup strawberry slices (luck, love)

Fresh mint sprigs for garnish (money, healing, purification)

Make just before serving. Prepare the fruit and add it to a punch bowl. Pour in the brandy and triple sec or liqueur (if used), then add the champagne (or ginger ale) and club soda. Stir lightly to combine and charge with intent. Either add a sprig of mint to each glass or float them in the bowl as garnish.

Incense

This incense is crafted to not only cleanse the atmosphere and bring renewal but also to offer the energy to help manifest our intent.

Unfolding Renewal Incense

1 tablespoon rosemary (purification, prosperity, love)

1 teaspoon orange zest (love, luck, money)

Pinch sage (wishes, prosperity)

Pinch cloves (love, protection, cleansing)

Combine the herbs in a bowl, mixing them with your fingers. Charge the incense with the energy of purification and happiness. Bottle and use as desired.

Incense Spell

In addition to using this incense as a general atmosphere cleanser, it can be used to amplify the intent of a New Year's resolution; transforming it from an affirmation exercise into a magical spell.

Unleashing the Resolve

Cauldron (or censer and heatproof dish)

1 incense charcoal

Unfolding Renewal incense

1 white candle

Paper and pen

Write what you resolve to accomplish in the new year on the piece of paper and mentally (and emotionally) pour all of your desire to achieve the goal or goals into it. Light the candle and also the charcoal in the cauldron and when it is glowing and ready, smolder the incense. Hold the paper in your hands visualizing yourself having accomplished your goal(s), then light the paper in the candle's flame and drop it in the cauldron over the incense (or on the dish) and say,

> *For good of all and by free will, let this magic now fulfill;*
> *what is sought shall be claimed,*
> *all goals are reached, even those unnamed;*
> *The work is done, the power set free,*
> *as I desire, so mote it be.*

Once the incense is completely cooled, bury the ashes in the ground or in a flowerpot.

Oils

This oil formula can be used to increase energy and shore up your motivation to follow through and achieve those New Year's resolutions magical or otherwise.

Get Up and Go Oil

1 tablespoon grapefruit zest (purification, healing, energy)

1 tablespoon ground coffee (energy, clarity)

½ cup corn oil (luck, protection)

¼ teaspoon sesame oil (opportunity, prosperity)

Add the grapefruit zest and coffee to the corn oil in a pot and warm over low heat until you can smell the aroma in the air. Remove from heat and allow to cool before adding the sesame oil. Strain, bottle, and charge with your intent.

Oil Spell

A good way to enhance your motivation to reach your goals is to work a bit of candle magic. This spell can be used to focus your energy and channel it into accomplishing your objectives. To have "fire in the belly" is an expression usually used to denote having the burning desire and determination to accomplish a goal. With magic, we can take this concept and go further than mere metaphor; we can infuse ourselves with that determination via the food we eat and the energy we channel and express.

Fire in the Belly

1 cupcake or slice of cake in your favorite flavor

1 white birthday candle

Get Up and Go oil

Have a prepared cupcake or slice of cake, homemade or store bought. Carefully anoint the birthday candle with a little bit of the oil; while holding it with your fingers, fill yourself with a sense of determination to reach whatever goal you have in mind and transfer this feeling into the candle. Press the candle halfway into the cupcake and visualize that as you do, the energy is charging the cake with your intent in a similar manner as an athame charging water in a cup. When you are ready, light the candle and to seal the spell say:

> *Flame of passion to reach my goal,*
> *brought to bear in this confection;*
> *I'm filled with desire evermore*
> *to achieve my purpose with new direction.*

Allow the candle to burn itself down to the cake and once it is out (snuff it with a spoon if necessary), eat a few bites of the cake to absorb the magic. Eat around the candle as much as you want, and then bury the remains in the ground or in a flowerpot.

Powders

When hosting a gathering such as a party for New Year's, an important consideration that can get easily overlooked in the frenzy of preparation is that of security. With so many people gathered together it can be difficult to weed out party crashers or unsavory people. Even if you aren't hosting an event, magical methods for warding away or dispelling unwelcome people or energies are always good to have on hand. Though this does count as a powder, it is not a typical formula. Chances are you already have these ingredients on hand.

SHIELD POWDER

¼ cup salt (protection, blessing)

¼ cup black pepper (protection, banishing)

Glass or ceramic salt/pepper shaker

Using a mortar and pestle, spice grinder, or coffee grinder, blend the salt and pepper together into fine powder. You may want to cover your mouth and nose with one of those surgical face masks people sometimes wear to avoid the flu as all the pepper can be irritating. After they have been blended pour the salt/pepper mixture into the shaker. Charge it with the energy of protection. When you wish to use this powder, sprinkle it from the shaker along the walls of each room indoors as if you are seasoning the perimeter of your home. To seal the intention, as you use the powder, say this spell:

> *Salt and pepper join together*
> *to keep me safe from harm,*
> *powerful magic weaves the shield;*
> *a circle of power around this home.*

Charms

Though charms are often thought of as bags of herbs or carefully crafted metal disks engraved with archaic sigils (both are powerful forms of magic), this charm is much more basic. But with determination, clear intention, and energy, it can be just as powerful.

Noisy New Year's Wish Charm

1 white candle

1 party horn noisemaker

Photo or drawing of your wish

Have a clear wish in mind before activating this as a charm. Ideally, obtain a photograph or drawing of what you wish or have something that symbolizes your wish to you. For the noisemaker, at this time of year there are usually multiple styles available. My favorite version is the blower type that unfurl as the noise is made but any style will do. Place the picture under the white candle. Light the candle, pick up the noisemaker, and focus all your energy and attention on your wish. Hold the noisemaker over the candle (high enough to avoid burning yourself, of course) and picture. Say:

> *To gain a wish on New Year's night,*
> *I place my intention into this charm;*
> *when the air is filled with cheerful noise,*
> *desire be granted with toot of horn!*

Extinguish the candle and wrap the horn in natural cloth, saving it until midnight.

As the time draws near, take out the horn and focus your thoughts on your wish. When midnight comes and it is time, blow the horn and visualize the energy being released to grant your wish; see the wish already fulfilled. Keep the horn as a keepsake until the magic manifests.

Foods

The celebration of New Year's Eve usually constitutes some form of party and a party usually calls for hors d' oeuvres. In keeping with the magical theme of this particular holiday, this appetizer is attuned to the power of success, transformation, and purification.

Magical Cheese Bites

8 ounces goat cheese (transformation, success, energy)

8 ounces cream cheese (transformation, success, happiness)

1 cup pistachios, shelled and ground
  (purification)

Melon baller or 1-teaspoon-sized
  measuring spoon

In a bowl, mash the cream cheese and goat cheese together
and once combined, cover with plastic wrap and chill for
half an hour. When ready, scoop out little balls of the cheese
mixture and roll them in the ground pistachios. Continue
until all the cheese has been used. Set the hors d' oeuvres
on their serving platter and charge them with intent before
serving.

Each season has an elemental influence that tends to
predominate, and many (if not most) practitioners believe
the earth element has the greatest influence for the season of winter. In winter, the earth in her dormant state is
very dominant. We can align with this energy for purification among other things. A brief but relevant digression is
needed here; each element has the ability to purify, albeit
through slightly different means. The purification of which
I speak is not to be rid of anything "sinful," "unclean," or
"evil," but rather a transformation of energies; freeing one-
self of anything that may be harmful or counterproductive
to your highest good. We strip the energy that is present of
any incorrect intentions, replacing them with the intention
of blessing. It is always best when removing or banishing
something (even "just" intention) to replace what is lost

with some form of blessing, lest any random vibe be drawn into the vacuum.

Returning to the subject at hand, the ideal purification for wintertime (also perfectly timed for the new calendar year) is to use a specially formulated bath salt. The ingredients of this bath salt formula are all rich and earthy and aid purification. Add it to a nice soak in a hot bath or put a handful of the salts in a washrag and use it to scrub your skin while showering. Incidentally, Epsom salt can usually be found in the health and beauty aisle of most supermarkets.

Bath Salts

The base for most bath salts is Epsom salt (a magnesium sulfate), sea salt or table salt, and a small bit of baking soda, which helps minimize any potential skin irritation.

Winter Purification Bath Salt

1½ cups sea salt

¾ cup Epsom salt

¼ cup baking soda

4 sprigs of fresh rosemary or a cheesecloth pouch
   filled with some dried rosemary (purification)

Canning jar or large bottle with tight-fitting lid

Mix the Epsom salt, sea salt, and baking soda in a bowl to combine. Place the rosemary into the jar and pour the salt mixture over it. Holding your hands over the jar, charge the bath salts with purification and blessing energies. Put the lid on the jar and store in a dry, dark place for at least three days to allow the salts to absorb some of the energy and fragrance from the rosemary. Use as desired.

Witch Bottles

This bottle is another that should be more of a diorama in that it should be constructed not only from the herbs and materials aligned with your intention, but also be constructed so that just by looking at it, you are reminded of your magical goal; the look of the witch bottle should be related to its purpose.

THREE REALMS BOTTLE

1 part coffee grounds (energy)

1 part raisins (abundance)

1 part sunflower seeds (luck, strength)

Large-mouthed bottle or canning jar with lid

Accessories aligned with your goal (see below)

Pour the ground coffee into the bottle. The coffee is not only to lend energy but also to represent the realm of Land. Layer the raisins over the coffee; the raisins correspond to the realm of Sea. Next, add the sunflower seeds which not only stand for the sun but also the realm of Sky. With the three realms in place, it is time to build your magical intent by adding ingredients that symbolize your goal. As an example, for love you could add sugar which is attuned to Venus, some cardamom, and two hearts cut from citrus peels that are then dried. Lemons are a bit more attuned to yin energies, oranges to yang, and limes could be used for anywhere along the spectrum. Personal items such as hair, nail clippings, or photographs can also be added at this time.

This bottle does not have to be limited to love magic; any goal can be built into the bottle. All that is needed is a goal and to look up what ingredients can be added that will match the goal. See the Ingredient Table of Correspondence list at the back of the book for ideas. Whatever goal is chosen, carefully craft a pleasant looking arrangement on top of the realm layers, summon up your energy, and charge the bottle with your intent. Place the lid on the bottle and to seal the spell, say the following (or something similar):

> *The three great realms of life combine*
> *and fuse with my magical intent.*
> *To bring about [state goal] divine,*
> *the bottle is sealed and message sent.*

Keep the bottle where you will be able to see it but it won't be disturbed by other people.

Witchy Ways

Nothing puts a damper on a holiday celebration like catching a cold. While science has yet to bless us with cures for the common cold or the flu, magically minded folks have come up with concoctions to "treat" or ward off illnesses, but as author Judika Illes reminds us, "healing spells are not intended to be used instead of conventional, traditional, or other methods of healing. Instead, they work best in conjunction with them, reinforcing other systems, enhancing their power and likelihood of recovery."[3] Making sure that there are no food allergies involved, using culinary herbs and ingredients in a healing practice is usually safe and sometimes surprisingly effective. Since this timeframe is deep into the cold of winter, it may be helpful to have a recipe for a food-based mixture to help strengthen the body and ward off sickness.

HEALING HERBAL HONEY

2 cups honey

4 tablespoons rosemary (purification, healing)

4 tablespoons garlic powder (healing, banishing)

2 teaspoons sage (cleansing, healing)

2 teaspoons oregano (healing, purification)

2 teaspoons thyme (healing, energy, purification)

1 teaspoon onion powder (healing)

---

3   Judika Illes, *The Element Encyclopedia of 1000 Spells* (New York: HarperElement, 2004), 334.

Warm the honey over low heat until it is just heated through. Remove from heat and stir the herbs into the honey before it cools. Pour the mixture into a clean mason jar or bottle and allow to cool before putting the lid on. At this time, charge the mixture with pure, white light for healing. After you put on the lid, store the honey in a cool, dark place such as a cabinet for two weeks to allow the ingredients to mingle, stirring occasionally to evenly distribute the herbs.

Once the honey is ready, it can be added to teas, sauces, salad dressings, cakes, or breads as needed for both flavor and magical healing energy. The honey can be stored in a cabinet or in the refrigerator.

New Year's Shopping List
- Baking soda
- Birthday candles (white)
- Brandy
- Cake
- Candles (white)
- Champagne
- Cloves
- Club soda
- Coffee
- Corn oil

- Cream cheese
- Epsom salt
- Goat cheese
- Grapefruit
- Lemons
- Limes
- Mint
- Oranges
- Party horn
- Pepper (black)
- Pineapple
- Pistachios
- Raisins
- Rosemary
- Sage
- Sea salt
- Sesame oil
- Strawberries
- Sunflower seeds
- Triple sec

CHAPTER 5

Emergence from The Gloom

In the summertime when you look to the western skies around nine o'clock at night, you can still see traces of daylight, that hazy orange color gradually fading into gray-ish blue, dark blue, and finally indigo as the last little sun rays slip from sight. During the winter, however, you are lucky if you can see any light in the sky past five o' clock. So much of the time in winter is spent in darkness that we can feel as though we are stuck in the gloom. Now that we have moved past the solstice and New Year's Day, the light hours of the day are beginning to become noticeably longer, and we begin to move back into a more active time.

Breaking Free

A key component of this time of the year is that though it begins in the darkness of winter, we must be quick to ready ourselves and prepare for the onset of spring. This is the time for quiet action; laying the groundwork for endeavors that we shall undertake as soon as the season permits. The most obvious agricultural way that we can participate in this trend is to plant seeds for vegetables, herbs, and flowers that we wish to grow throughout spring and summer. Seeds and starter pots are just beginning to be sold in many places or if not yet, will soon be available.

If you would like to plant a few seeds for herbs to use in future magic in starter trays, you can use this small ritual in order to encourage healthy growth.

Seeds of Unfolding Potential

1 packet unflavored gelatin (binding, sealing)

1 cup hot water

3 cups cold water

Packet of seeds

Seed starter trays (or small flowerpots)

Potting soil

Dissolve the gelatin in the cup of hot water and then combine with the cold water, stirring to blend. Charge the water with your intent that the seeds it nourishes will grow in strength and power. Plant the seeds in the starter trays and as you sprinkle them with the gelatin water, say this spell, "Filled with promise, seeds sprout forth; vitality unleashed with magical growth." Tend to them with loving care and they will surely grow in robust health and magic.

Simmering Potpourris

This time of the year, with its emergence from the darkest portion of winter and promise of spring to come, is a phase of enormous potential. With so much of the world in the initial stages of creation, we too can be inspired to extend our own creativity and begin new projects now. This potpourri helps to charge the atmosphere with the energies conducive to inspiration and creativity.

Inspiration Potpourri

1 whole orange (solar energy)

2 tablespoon coffee grounds (energy, clarity)

1 teaspoon sage, dried (cleansing, clarity)

Water

Fill a pot about half full with water. Peel the orange and toss the peelings into the pot. Break the orange into segments and add these to the pot as well. Next, sprinkle in the coffee and the sage. Charge the ingredients with the intention that they will aid inspiration and creativity. Turn on the stove. Allow the pot to simmer for as long as desired, adding more water as needed.

Brews

There are times when even a magically charged environment may not bring all the inspiration we need. Lack of sleep, too many daily chores, a looming deadline, just plain stress, or a host of other reasons can cloud our minds and seemingly disconnect us from the creative flow. When I find myself staring blankly at a half-finished project, I turn to magic for assistance in jump-starting my right-brained, artistic side. This brew is a nice method of helping to tap into that energy. Inspiration has been a serious pursuit of many over the centuries and can even be seen in the tales of heroes and deities.

Looking to the Welsh tales of Taliesin, we are shown Cerridwen, a mighty being of great magical prowess. In her cauldron she was creating an enchanted brew of *awen* (divine poetic inspiration or "flowing spirit") in order to grant her son Avagddu (the most ill-favored man in the world) great wisdom so that he would be admitted in the company of the men of noble birth. For this delicate brew, she studied books of astronomers and planetary hours and gathered charm-bearing herbs for a year and a day. Three drops of this brew were mistakenly consumed by Gwion Bach, the young boy Cerridwen left to stir the cauldron, granting him great wisdom. Long story short, a magical battle ensued between Gwion Bach and Cerridwen that resulting in him being consumed by her—he as a grain of wheat and she as a black hen. Later (in her normal form) she gave (re)birth to him, but now he had become Taliesin, ("shining brow") who would become a legendary bard.[4]

Using this magical tale as a guide, it is clear to see the significance inspiration can hold. In this era, we can create our own potions of inspiration in a much simpler fashion. My recipe for this potion is a little less involved than gathering herbs over the course of a year and a day; one trip to the grocery store should be sufficient! Much like Cerridwen did, I use planetary information as my guide. In my recipe, I add an enchanted ingredient aligned with each of the classical seven planets known to the ancients: the Sun, Mercury, Venus, the Moon, Mars, Jupiter, and Saturn. These ingredients are also naturally aligned to inspiration, memory, clear thought, healing, purification, and love, creating a powerful brew designed to clear the mental cobwebs and make way for fresh insights, flashes of genius, and a brand new vision toward familiar tasks. The power of this potion also helps to attune us to the inspirational energies of Imbolc.

Cauldron of Inspiration Potion

1 teaspoon rosemary (for the Sun)

1 teaspoon sage (for Jupiter)

---

4   Lady Charlotte Guest, translator, *The Mabinogion: Translated from the Red Book of Hergest*. (Mineola, NY: Dover Publications, 1997. Originally published 1877), 471–473.

1 teaspoon mint (for Mercury)

1 teaspoon grapefruit zest (for Saturn)

1 teaspoon basil (for Mars)

1 teaspoon lemon juice (for the Moon)

1 tablespoon honey (for Venus)

2 cups water

Charge each of the herbs and the honey separately for inspiration. In a cauldron or pot, heat the water to just under the boiling point when little bubbles appear at the bottom of the pot and steam begins to rise. Add the herbs one at a time and allow the brew to come to a boil. After the pot is fully boiling, turn off the heat and cover the pot. Allow the brew to steep and cool for at least 15 minutes. Uncover the pot and stir in the honey. Pour a cup of the brew, straining it if necessary, and relax as you take slow sips of the potion allowing your mind to open to wisdom.

Holiday: Imbolc

Imbolc, Imbolg, Brigid's Day, Candlemas…there are many names for this sabbat. Though it is well known that this day has been celebrated for centuries, little is known of actual ancient practices, possibly due to the fact that it occurs during one of the coldest parts of the year in the Northern Hemisphere. What is generally known is that it is a time to seek divination of the spring weather; clean; tend to hearth, home, and self; and also celebrate the sun with fire and honor deities, particularly the goddess Brigid.[5] This holiday has traditionally (again, probably due to the cold) been more of a "stay at home" type of celebration rather than the big outdoor revelries found at the warmer sabbats.

Relighting the hearth-fire; preparing a feast; cleaning the house; ritualistically washing the head, hands, and feet for purification; divination not only for upcoming weather but also for the full season, and honoring the goddess with such items as Brigid's crosses are all traditionally sound customs. I will include a full nondenominational ritual for celebrating Imbolc later in this chapter.

Incense

This incense would also be a boon to inspiration and creativity but is specifically intended for the sabbat of Imbolc.

IMBOLC INCENSE

2 chamomile tea bags (peace, solar energy)

1 teaspoon rosemary (solar energy, purification)

1 teaspoon sage (cleansing)

1 bay leaf, crumbled (solar energy, purification)

---

5 Janet and Stewart Farrar, *A Witches Bible Compleat*, (New York: Magickal Childe, 1984), 61–65.

Break open the chamomile tea bags into a bowl. Add the remaining ingredients, mix them together with your fingers, and charge the incense for inspiration and strength. Bottle for use.

Incense Spell

This spell is designed to magically assist new projects and endeavors. If you are trying to create something new—start a business, write a book, learn to play a musical instrument, or things of that nature and you would like a magical edge, this spell can help.

Smoke of Intent

Imbolc incense

1 white candle

Paper

Pen

Incense charcoal

Cauldron or heatproof dish

Write your intention (what you wish to create) on the paper. Light the white candle. In the cauldron, light the charcoal and when it is glowing, add a bit of the incense. Pick up the paper and envision your goal strongly as if it has already manifested. Fill yourself with how you want to feel when your wish has been achieved and mentally transfer this energy into the paper. Light the paper in the flame of the candle and drop it into the cauldron over the incense and say the spell:

> *Smoke and flame, release my intent,*
> *shape this goal with magic petition.*
> *Through mystical realms, the power is sent,*
> *to bring my desire into fruition.*

Allow the incense and candle to burn out on their own if possible, but snuff out the candle if necessary. When everything has cooled, bury the ashes in the ground or a flowerpot. You could also place the ashes in a black magic pouch to carry the remnants as a charm.

Oils

This oil recipe is designed to align with the energy of Imbolc. When charging it with energy, visualize the sun rising up over snow covered mountains to help capture the spirit of the holiday.

Imbolc Sun Oil

1 teaspoon sage (cleansing)

1 teaspoon sunflower seeds (strength)

1 chamomile tea bag (solar energy)

½ cup olive oil or almond oil (peace, prosperity)

Open the tea bag and empty its contents into a pot. Add the oil, sunflower seeds, and sage, and warm over low heat until you can smell the herbs in the air. Allow to cool for at least 15 minutes, strain, charge with intent, and bottle for use.

Oil Spell

This spell is fast, simple, and effective in clearing away incorrect vibes and filling yourself with harmonious energies.

Self-Blessing

Imbolc Sun oil

Anoint your wrists, forehead, and back of the neck with the oil. If you feel particularly ill at ease, you can also anoint your solar plexus, back of the knees, and bottoms of your feet with the oil. Visualize the sun rising over snowy mountains as you did to charge the oil initially, but now also see the sunlight shining down upon yourself. As the light touches your skin, it actually shines through you, filling your body with blessed energy while at the same time casting out anything that is not in harmony with you. Hold the visualization for as long as desired.

Powders

This powder can be used to help access the unknown. There are two ways to use it. The first way is to use it as an actual divination medium by pouring some of the powder onto a plate, closing your eyes, running your finger through it randomly, and then looking for symbols in the tracings. The second method is to use the powder to encircle candles or divinatory tools in order to enhance their effectiveness.

Divination Powder

1 tablespoon mustard seed (protection)

1 tablespoon sage (clarity, cleansing)

1 tablespoon caraway seed (protection)

1 tablespoon nutmeg (psychic awareness)

1 tablespoon lemongrass (psychic awareness)

Grind all of the ingredients together into a fine powder. Charge the powder with your intent for psychic awareness and bottle for use.

Charms

To develop a deeper connection with the sabbats, some Witches create special charms attuned to a holiday's energy and either carry them or hang them up in their homes for the length of the season. To create a charm for Imbolc, you can make an herbal sachet.

Imbolc Charm Bag

Cheesecloth

Kitchen twine or white thread

1 teaspoon sage, dried (cleansing, clarity)

1 teaspoon rose petals, dried (love,
  psychic awareness)

1 chamomile tea bag (solar energy)

3 hazelnuts (wisdom)

Fold the cheesecloth in half and fill with the herbs. Roses are usually available in supermarkets this time of year because of Valentine's Day. A single flower should be sufficient. Charge the mixture using the same visualization of the sun rising over snow covered mountains from the Imbolc Sun oil instructions. Bundle up the cheesecloth around the herbs and tie it shut with the twine, leaving a length of twine for hanging. Cut any loose ends and hang up where desired.

Foods

This time of year is traditionally associated with sheep, ewe's milk, and baby lambs, so as far as food is concerned, roast lamb and dairy foods are prominent. Spicy foods are also appropriate at this time in honor of the strengthening sun. This recipe will be a slight departure from those foods and can be easily modified for vegetarians or vegans thanks to the number of meat substitutes on the market as well as sour cream alternatives made from soy beans or even cashews available today.

Imbolc Shepard's Pie

3 cups potatoes, mashed

2 cups cooked meat, ground (beef, lamb, etc.)

1 cup mixed vegetables, frozen

½ teaspoon garlic, minced

1 onion, chopped

2 tablespoons vegetable oil (or use cooking spray)

3 tablespoons sour cream (or vegan substitute)

½ teaspoon sage

Salt and pepper

Preheat oven to 425° F. Sauté the onion and garlic in a pan with the oil or spray until softened (about 4 to 5 minutes). Add the sage and salt and pepper to taste. Brown the meat and remove from heat. If you would like to substitute the meat, you can either omit it entirely or swap out some vegetarian ground meat substitute. Next, stir in the vegetables and sour cream. Pour into a greased 2-quart baking pan (8-inch square or 7x11-inch rectangle pan). Top with the mashed potatoes. You can use the tines of a fork to decorate the top with magical symbols, a sun disk, or simply draw zigzags or lines through the potatoes. Bake in the oven until the tops of the potatoes are browned; about 10 to 15 minutes.

Ritual

Key traditional factors for Imbolc can frequently include purification in some form, fire in some form, and using magic to "turn the wheel" to quicken the coming of spring.

In many traditions, the goddess Brigid is honored at this time. This is a cross quarter day, meaning that it falls (roughly) in the middle of the four traditional calendar seasons; a pivotal time when the first stirrings of spring are sought in hopes of a fruitful year. The following ritual will address these time-honored practices in a more modern context.

Imbolc Winter Rose Ritual

1 long-stemmed red rose

Cauldron (or flowerpot), filled with soil

Chalice of water

Athame

8 tea light candles (white)

Bowl of ice

Bowl of water

Empty bowl

Bowl with red candle

The framework of this ritual is to honor the cold of winter while channeling the elements into the center point to turn the wheel toward spring. A rose should, as previously stated, be available in most supermarkets at this time of year. If a rose cannot be obtained for some reason, a wand or a whole red apple are appropriate substitutes. Prior to the ritual, clean the ritual area and set up everything. Place the cauldron in the center on an altar table and surround it with the eight white candles. The chalice of water goes on the left side of the altar and the athame goes on the right side. Set the bowl of ice to the north, the "empty" bowl to the east, the bowl with the unlit red candle to the south and the bowl of water to the west. Now that everything is set up, bathe with the intent of purification, taking special care to wash your head, hands, and feet.

After the bath, dress as desired and return to the ritual area, carrying the rose (or substitute). Drive the stem of the rose into the soil in the cauldron deep enough that it will stand upright. Light the red candle in the south and each of the white tea lights around the cauldron. Pick up the athame and starting in the north, trace a circle of energy around the working area. Walk the circle three times; ending in the north declaring, "Only energies in harmony with me may enter this circle." Call out to the energies of the earth element saying, "power of earth, frozen in slumber; awaken and return; vital and strong." Move to the east and call out to the air, "power of air, cold winter winds; rush through the skies and hasten the change." At the south say, "power of fire, burgeoning sun; increase in energy and life-giving power." Finally, in the west say, "power of water, elixir of life; surge forth in strength and nourish the land."

Returning to the altar, tap the cauldron three times with the athame and say, "Elements all, hear my word; fertilize the land and enliven the earth. I call to the center the sacred powers to enchant this rose as Witch's flower." Visualize that the earth, air, fire, and water energies are being drawn from the quarters to the center forming a solar cross within the circle and charging the rose with their power. Now is the time to call upon deities. If you are working with a goddess and god, you could call them by saying:

> *Goddess of the land, winter's red rose;*
> *come to me now, back from repose,*
> *bless the earth vital and new,*
> *restoring the light, shining and true.*
> *God of light, promise, and growth;*
> *return to the earth, please come forth,*
> *he who is reborn and waxing in power,*
> *nurture the life of animal, plant, seed, and flower.*

Pick up the athame in one hand and the chalice of water in the other. Lower the blade into the chalice and say:

> *Vessel of creation, waters of life,*
> *union of spirit and flesh combine,*
> *liquid charged through cup and knife,*
> *nourish the earth, bless, and align.*

Set down the athame and hold the cup in both hands, taking a sip of the water in reverence then say: "Blessed be the earth, blessed be the sun, may Imbolc bring fruitful renewal to all. So mote it be."

Pour some of the water into the cauldron, watering the rose as if it were a houseplant.

If you have any spells, petitions, or prayers to conduct, now is the time to work them. If you are ready to conclude the rite, thank the deities for their presence in your own words and then go to the western quarter. Thank the water energy for its presence then move to the south, thanking the fire energy. Move to the east thanking the air energy and finally, end in the north thanking the energy of the earth. Pick up the athame and again, moving counter-clockwise, draw in the circle of energy to open the circle and release your intent. Conclude by saying, "This circle is open and set free, my rite is ended, blessed be." Afterward, have a feast of a meal in honor of Imbolc.

Witchy Ways

Even though this time traditionally celebrates the return of the sun and warmth, in many places the actual weather is still quite cold. If this is the case where you live, it may feel difficult to connect to the heat of the sun during ritual or just in general. If this is so, it might be helpful to begin a meditative practice of sitting where the sun filters through a window, closing your eyes, and visualizing the sun's rays pouring down upon you, vitalizing your psychic centers and nourishing your astral body with its light. A regular sun meditation can be an energy boost and an aid to good health.

Imbolc Shopping List

- Almond oil

- Basil

- Bay leaves

- Candles (white and red)

- Caraway seeds

- Chamomile tea

- Cheesecloth

- Coffee

- Garlic

- Gelatin (unflavored)

- Grapefruit

- Hazelnuts

- Honey

- Kitchen twine (or thread)

- Lemons

- Lemongrass

- Meat

- Mint

- Mixed vegetables (frozen)

- Mustard seeds

- Nutmeg
- Olive oil
- Onion
- Orange
- Pepper
- Potatoes
- Potting soil
- Rosemary
- Roses
- Sage
- Salt
- Seeds
- Seed starter trays
- Sour cream
- Sunflower seeds

CHAPTER 6

Hearts and Flowers

The middle of February heralds the arrival of the "holiday of love," Valentine's Day. The stores become filled with heart-shaped boxes of candy, stuffed animals, romantic greeting cards, and lots and lots of roses. Since this day is so prominent in our society and love spells are such a large focus of magical practice, this chapter on Valentine's Day is needed.

HOLIDAY: Valentine's Day

Looking at this holiday, we see three possible options: Focusing on the possible Pagan origins of the day as being a Christianized form of Lupercalia, a Roman holiday that was celebrated in the middle of February; focusing on "Saint Valentine" and one of the legends surrounding his connection to the holiday; or focusing on the holiday as its modern secular incarnation—a day dedicated to romance. Addressing the first point; the ancient Roman holiday of Lupercalia was a purification and fertility holiday where the priests, adorned in goat hide, struck passersby with goatskin straps and those struck were thereby believed to become more fertile as a result.[6] The second point, regarding the actual Saint Valentine; there are actually several Saint Valentines identified by the Catholic Church. Legend has it that "the" Saint Valentine was either an early Christian priest who married young couples even though it was forbidden by the Roman emperor to do so, or that he was imprisoned and fell in love with his jailor's daughter. Eventually his legend grew and he became the patron saint of lovers.[7] The third option and my preferred focus is to just celebrate the day as it is now, a day for love.

Simmering Potpourris

To create an environment filled with loving and romantic energy, this potpourri bubbling on the stove with its sweetly-scented steam drifting into the air is a fantastic first step.

Aura of Romance Potpourri

1 tablespoon coriander seeds (love, lust)

---

6   Janet and Stewart Farrar, *A Witches Bible Compleat,* (New York: Magickal Childe, 1984), 65.

7   Jeannie Meekins, *Saint Valentine: The Man Who Became the Patron Saint of Love* (Learning Island.com, 2013), 1–5.

1 tablespoon cardamom (love)

1 teaspoon cinnamon (love)

1 apple, sliced (love)

Red wine (or water)

Fill a pot about halfway with the wine or water. Add the apple slices and the spices and charge the ingredients with the intention to fill the atmosphere with loving energies. Turn on the stove and allow the pot to simmer for as long as desired, adding more wine or water as needed.

Brews
Far from the notion of an evil old crone giving a young person a vial of mysterious liquid then used to enchant the object of their affections, most potions today are not designed to dominate the will of another. Many potions are worn rather than ingested in order to yield their influence. The potion included here is meant to be drunk, but not as a magically compulsory elixir. It is meant to enhance already present feelings according to free will. It also works well as a libation during love spells or as a general mood enhancer. In my experience, its effects last for about an hour and a half.

BUBBLING LOVE POTION
1 cup apple juice (love)

2 teaspoons basil (love)

1 teaspoon cloves (love, lust)

½ cup water (love)

1 cup club soda (energy enhancer)

2 teaspoons sugar (love) or stevia sweetener (success)

Chill the club soda and apple juice. Pour the water into a pot and add the cloves and basil. Simmer the mixture just until it starts to boil. You'll definitely be able to smell it in the air. Remove from heat and strain it through a sieve into a cup. Using one of those permanent filters from a coffee pot is a good idea. You can buy a spare one and use it exclusively for things like this. Stir in the sugar and allow it to cool. Once cooled, pour in the apple juice and charge with the intent that "This potion shall enhance the love already felt between those that drink it, according to free will and for the good of all." Add the club soda and serve.

Incense

The drifting, curling smoke of this incense can fill the air with just the right energy for love. With a spicy scent and associations with the air and fire elements, this incense brings forth a strong vibration of sexy romance.

Fiery Enchantment Incense

1 tablespoon basil (love)

1 tablespoon marjoram (love)

1 tablespoon rosemary (love)

1 teaspoon tarragon (love)

Grind the herbs together and charge them with intent. Bottle the incense for use.

Incense Spell
Similar to smudging the air to be rid of difficult energy patterns, you can infuse the atmosphere with energy geared toward any desire, as in this spell.

Charging the Air for Romance
Fiery Enchantment incense

Incense charcoal

Incense burner (that can be carried)

Matches or lighter

If you are going out—especially on a date and are going to be picked up—and you are looking to enhance the romantic potential of your evening, this spell can be cast in your home filling the area and surrounding yourself with the ideal energy. If you do not have access to an incense burner that can be carried around, you can use a heatproof bowl filled halfway with sand or salt to hold the charcoal and carry it around.

Light the charcoal, place it in the incense burner, and when it is glowing and ready, sprinkle on the incense. Carry the burner around your home moving clockwise, and focus on feeling romantic. Let this feeling envelop you as you go from room to room. Pay special attention to the living room and bedroom, and hold the incense over the outfit that you will wear. After you have completed the circuit, allow the incense to burn out in the living room and seal the intent with this spell:

> *Twisting and curling in magical dance,*
> *infused and aligned for love and affection;*
> *enchanted smoke of tender romance,*
> *fill the air with my intention!*

Make sure the charcoal is completely out and cooled (putting it in water if necessary) before you go out for the evening.

Oils

A dab of a magical oil designed for love on each wrist, the third eye point on your forehead, and the back of your neck are all that is needed to surround yourself with an aura of attraction you carry with you wherever you go. Beyond this, the oil can also be used to anoint spell candles, love letters, or charms to radiate a loving vibration.

Apple Pie Love Oil

Peel from one apple (love)

2½ tablespoons pumpkin pie spice (love, lust)

½ cup olive oil (peace)

First, peel the skin from one apple. It does not have to be done very carefully or in one single strip or anything. You can even use a cheese grater if you don't mind a lot of juice everywhere. Place the peels in a pot. Next, add the pumpkin pie spice. If you cannot find premade pumpkin pie spice, you can mix your own by blending together 1 tablespoon cinnamon, 1 teaspoon ginger, 1 teaspoon nutmeg, ¾ teaspoon allspice, and ¾ teaspoon cloves. Pour the oil into the pot over the peelings and spices, and simmer over very low heat, stirring a little if needed. Remove from heat after you can smell the herbs in the air and allow the oil to cool. Once cooled, charge the oil for love, strain, and bottle it for use.

OIL SPELL

This spell can be used to find a new love; it is a call for a compatible partner and is not designed to be cast "on" someone specific. Prior to casting this spell, find a suitable tree that you can (for lack of a better word) befriend and return to often. Ideally, a fruit tree such as apple, peach, or apricot but any tree that makes you feel comfortable will do. Visit the tree and give it water, talk to it, ask it if it will accept being part of your spell. If you feel uneasy, rejected, or "strange" around the tree after asking, then it is best to find a new tree. Once you have connected to the correct tree and established a bit of a rapport, then cast this spell. Do not substitute an unknown oil for this spell. The ingredients of the oil called for in the spell contain only safe substances.

Love in Every Realm

1 cup water

1 tablespoon Apple Pie Love oil

Bring the tree an offering of water with a tablespoon of the love oil stirred into it. Focus strongly on how you want to feel when you have found new love and the type of person you would like to meet. As you pour the water at the base of the tree, say this spell either out loud or simply think it strongly.

> *Sacred tree, reaching through realms divine,*
> *For strong relationship, I no longer wait;*
> *Draw new love, romance be mine,*
> *Send the message to a compatible mate.*
> *Forged in magic, by free will,*
> *Let this wish be fulfilled.*

Thank the tree for its assistance and continue to visit it and care for it as a magical ally.

Powders

Love powder sounds odd, doesn't it? It does to me at least, but it is useful to have around to encircle candles as a power boost, to use in magic bags as a quick charm, or in the love-themed magical project I include.

FIRE OF DESIRE POWDER

1 tablespoon cinnamon (love)

1 tablespoon unsweetened cocoa powder (love)

1 tablespoon coffee, ground (energy enhancer)

Combine the ingredients in a bowl or use a mortar and pestle or coffee grinder to blend all the powders into one. Charge the powder with your desire and bottle for use.

POWDER SPELL
Valentine to Yourself

1 piece construction paper, cardboard, or a plate

Fire of Desire powder

White household glue

Glue stick

If you decide to use a plate, make sure that it is one that you don't mind ruining for all other uses. You can get a little plate from a dollar store fairly easily which would be ideal. For the construction paper, the colors should be either pink or red and it should be cut into a circle. If cardboard is used, it too should be circular and painted in one of the appropriate colors.

Using the glue stick, outline a heart and any other symbols you'd like on the surface of the chosen item. Fill in the outlines with a thin layer of the household glue. Cover the entire surface with a dusting of the Fire of Desire powder and leave it to dry overnight. The next day, on a covered work surface, gently tap the item so that the excess powder falls off. This should leave a powder-covered design on the item. Holding the item in your hands, envision yourself filled with pink light, an irresistible aura of happiness and attraction surrounding you and drawing in love. Mentally infuse this feeling into the item as well, charging it as a love talisman. Store this where you will see it often but it won't be seen by random people. It can also be kept on an altar particularly during other love magic.

Charms

A simple, natural charm to bring love to you that would only seem slightly odd if found by another person is a magically charged nut. The Brazil nut is naturally infused with energy that brings luck in love. When magically transformed into a talisman, it can keep you surrounded by the energy of attraction for compatible people.

Love in a Nutshell

Fiery Enchantment incense

Incense charcoal

Incense burner

Apple Pie Love oil

1 Brazil nut (love)

1 pink candle

1 red candle

1 cup water or Bubbling Love potion

Bowl of salt or a pentacle

On a table or countertop, arrange an altar with the red candle on the left, the pink candle on the right, and the salt or pentacle in the middle. Set the cup of water in front of the red candle and the incense burner in front of the pink candle. Have the Brazil nut in the middle in front of the salt, and the bottle of oil in front of that, closest to you. Using the oil, anoint the candles, from the top to the middle and from the bottom to the middle. Light the charcoal and when it is glowing, add the incense.

After completing your preferred method of pre-ritual preparation such as a circle casting, light the candles, red and pink respectively. Hold the Brazil nut in your hands and will that it be free from any energies not in harmony with your goal then touch it lightly to the salt or pentacle. Again holding it, focus strongly on your magical intention; infuse this vision and feeling into the nut and anoint it with a drop of water and a drop of oil. Hold it over the smoke of the incense and finally high over the flame of the red and then pink candles.

Press the nut to your heart and say this spell to seal the intent: "By each element, earth, water, air, and fire, infuse this charm with my desire; gift from earth, draw love to me, as I will so mote it be." Drink a sip of the water (or potion) in thanks before ending the ritual. Extinguish the candles and the incense and pour the remainder of the water onto the earth. Carry the charm with you as much as possible when looking for new love.

Foods

Any of the standard aphrodisiac foods could be used for a nice Valentine's Day dinner provided that no one involved has an allergy to the ingredients. Nothing shifts focus away from a night of passionate romance faster than anaphylactic shock! Whether it's oysters, chocolate-covered strawberries, honey-dipped figs, or the cake in the following recipe, just make sure that the foods you include are safe, well-prepared, and delicious in order to create a meal most enchanting.

HONEY-BUTTER APPLESAUCE CAKE

3 cups flour (abundance, fertility)

2 cups light brown sugar, packed (love)

¼ cup honey (love)

2 cups chunky applesauce (love)

2 eggs (fertility, rejuvenation)

1 teaspoon salt (blessing)

1½ teaspoons cinnamon (love)

¼ teaspoon cardamom (love, lust)

¼ cup Apple Pie Love oil, plus a
little extra for the pan

¾ cup butter (transformation)

Preheat the oven to 350° F. If you can find a heart-shaped pan (9- or 10-inch) that would be ideal but any shaped pan will do: round; square; tube; etc. In a large mixing bowl, stir the flour, salt, baking soda, cardamom, and cinnamon together. In a separate bowl and with an electric mixer or wire whisk, beat butter, honey, eggs, and brown sugar together until combined and fluffy. Stir in the flour mixture until just combined, then add the Love oil and applesauce.

Grease the pan with the little extra Love oil or some cooking spray. Whether or not it is heart-shaped, trace a heart in the oil on the pan, mentally charging it with love energy, and then pour the batter into the pan. Bake in the oven 55 to 60 minutes until a knife inserted in the cake comes out mostly clean. Remove from oven and cool in the pan on a wire rack 15 minutes or until the pan is cool to the touch. Invert the pan on a cookie sheet to turn out the cake and then flip it onto its serving platter so it is right-side up. Frost with store-bought cream cheese frosting, leave plain, or dust the cake with powdered sugar as desired. Serve to enhance the feeling of love and happiness.

Bath Salts
Part of the preliminary work before going out to socialize usually includes a shower or bath. This can be a wonderful

first step in the magical process as well. The bath salts presented here can be used as a way to shift your energy and focus prior to casting a love spell and also during the interim as you are seeking its result.

Apple Pie Bath Salts

½ ounce Apple Pie Love oil

1½ cups sea salt

¾ cup Epsom salt

¼ cup baking soda

Mason jar (3 cup or larger)

Combine the Epsom salt, baking soda, and sea salt. Add the oil and stir. Hold your hands over the jar and infuse the salts with your desire. Put the lid on the jar and store in a dry, dark place for at least three days to allow the salts to absorb some of the energy and fragrance of the magical oil. Use as desired.

Witch Bottles

The purpose of a witch bottle is to act as a magical battery. Even the ancient recipes designed to protect from "evil witchcraft" were a type of battery in that they continually transmitted their intent on their own after their creation. The bottles are a larger incarnation of talismans. A bottle crafted to bring or enhance love is a spell enacted to project its energy continually so that a steady shift is enjoyed.

It is not "bam, pow!"-high drama magic to force love but instead is a permanent improvement in that area of life; a special advantage, so to speak.

ELEMENTS OF VENUS BOTTLE

¼ cup dried apricots (water)

¼ cup dried cranberries (fire)

½ cup honey (earth)

4 tablespoons tarragon (air)

Mason jar, 12-ounce

1 pink candle

Fiery Enchantment incense (optional)

Each of the ingredients for this bottle are aligned with the planet Venus and the goal of love. Though related to Venus, each resonates to a different element, and with the four elements of earth, air, fire, and water all represented they combine in this bottle to form a complete magical intention. To begin, wash and dry the mason jar and lid. Charge the pink candle with your desire and light it and the incense if used.

Layer the ingredients into the jar starting with the apricots, then the cranberries. Pour the honey into the bottle over the dried fruits and top with the tarragon. The herb is not only aligned to love, but the green color is one of the colors of Venus, its planetary ruler, making it doubly beneficial. Charge the open jar with your intent and then screw the lid on tight to contain the magic. Seal the lid by carefully dripping wax from the pink candle onto it in a clockwise circular pattern until the top is covered. Once the jar is sealed, hold it in your hands and once more focus on your desire while saying the spell to bind the intention.

> *Through power of Venus, vibration surge,*
> *water, fire, earth and air;*
> *charged with desire, together merge,*
> *encouraging love beyond compare;*
> *for good of all, with harm to none,*
> *I seal this bottle, the spell has begun.*

Place the bottle near your bed where it can radiate its influence while you sleep. If the bottle should ever spoil (though the honey helps discourage that), unseal the bottle, bury its contents deep in the ground, discard the jar, and create a new witch bottle using entirely new ingredients.

Witchy Ways

Not everything has to be made from scratch in order to be given magical intent. For Valentine's Day, a box of chocolates can be purchased and charged with loving energies. Simply trace a heart over the box with the first two fingers of your dominant hand and visualize pink, green, or copper colored light pouring into the candy, filling it with love magic. These chocolates can be shared with a loved one to build the emotional bond between the two of you or eaten by friends and family to increase love and friendship in general.

Valentine's Day Shopping List

- Apples
- Apple juice
- Applesauce
- Apricots, dried
- Baking soda
- Basil
- Brazil nuts
- Butter
- Candles (pink and red)
- Cardamom
- Cinnamon
- Cloves
- Club soda
- Cocoa powder (unsweetened)
- Coffee
- Coriander
- Cranberries, dried
- Eggs
- Epsom salt
- Flour

- Glue
- Glue stick
- Honey
- Marjoram
- Mason jars
- Olive oil
- Plate (or construction paper)
- Pumpkin pie spice
- Rosemary
- Sea salt
- Sugar (or stevia)
- Sugar, brown
- Tarragon
- Wine (red)

SECTION 2

SPRING
FORWARD

The orbit of the earth continues in its path and the polar tilt shifts back so that the sun is once again positioned over the equator. The snows of winter begin to melt, light mellow breezes replace fiercely cold winds, and the land starts to warm and awaken, bringing forth a vast array of new life in both the plant and animal worlds—and beyond.

CHAPTER 7

Power of Spring

The season of spring shares its primary characteristic with its opposite season, autumn. While summer marks the point in the year where the earth is positioned so the majority of the sun's rays are angled over one of the hemispheres (northern or southern, depending), the season of spring and autumn occur due to the exact same phenomenon; the sun's rays being primarily over the equator. What gives them their power is not only how the season is initiated but also what came before and what will happen after, underscoring the importance of the equinox days as times of balance. It is at the times of balance when the greatest potential for change occurs. During spring, with its balance of heat, light, and weather, the proper conditions are established to sustain the delicate unfolding of nature's new life. Tiny seedlings and baby animals can grow during this milder time before the full force of summer is upon them. I am of course speaking in ideal conditions; there are many times and places that do not experience the same thing. There are also plants and animals born at all times of the year, but for the vast majority of crops and domestic animals, this cycle is a needed advantage in their growth process.

The greatest power of spring is that of balance. It is such an important time, a phase of moderate temperatures as sweet relief from icy chills of winter and comfortable preparation for rising heat in summer. In this moment of temperance, we can gather our strength, shift our focus, and align with our goals. We unite our hopes with our potential, bringing fantastic achievements.

Growth and Abundance

A great deal of magic is centered around correspondences and sympathetic connections. Sympathetic magic is the style focused on the idea that things which share a similar nature can affect one another. Using a poppet to magically affect a person is a good example of this type of work. A broader example is timing your magical work to the phases of the moon or the changes in season. Since spring is the time of growth and (hopefully) increasing abundance in the natural world, it corresponds well to prosperity magic as well as working for long-term projects or to improve your luck.

Simmering Potpourris

With the scent of this potpourri drifting into the air, the energy shifts, clearing away those not in harmony with abundance and increasing your ability to gain and maintain prosperity.

PROSPERITY POTPOURRI

2 chamomile tea bags (money, peace)

2 tablespoons basil (money)

2 tablespoons rosemary (money, protection)

½ teaspoon ginger (money, power)

1 orange, sliced (money)

Water

Combine the first five ingredients into a pot. Hold your hands over the pot and charge the herbs with your intent for prosperity. Add enough water to cover the herbs and turn on the stove. Let the potpourri simmer for as long as desired, adding water if the level gets too low.

Brews

Earl Grey tea is traditionally made from regular black tea, (associated with money magic) and essential oil of bergamot (a citrus fruit with the Latin name *Citrus bergamia*) which is also aligned with money and prosperity. I enjoy the flavor of Earl Grey, but some do not care for the bergamot note. If that is the case, you can substitute regular tea for this potion.

Simple Money Potion

1 Earl Grey tea bag (money)

3 basil leaves (money)

Sugar, honey, or stevia sweetener (money)

Water

Place the basil leaves in the bottom of a tea cup and add the tea bag. Heat the water just under the boiling point and then pour into the cup. Allow the tea to steep for a few minutes, then remove the bag and basil leaves. Stir in the desired amount of sweetener and charge with the desire for money and prosperity.

Incense

Though this incense is made for the spring equinox, its energies are also useful for protection and healing.

Green Spring Incense

1 tablespoon marjoram (healing, protection)

1 tablespoon thyme (healing, purification)

1 teaspoon tarragon (protection, purification)

Grind the herbs together and to charge the incense visualize the sun shining down on a field of flowers, basking in the warmth and light. Mentally pour this energy into the incense and bottle for use.

Oils

The spicy yet flowery fragrance of this oil is a lovely magical accompaniment to equinox workings. It energy is naturally attuned to the spring and also lends itself well to prosperity magic.

Spring Equinox Oil

¼ cup almond oil (prosperity)

¼ cup olive oil (peace, good luck)

2 chamomile tea bags (money, peace, love)

1 tablespoon radish greens (protection, love)

½ teaspoon thyme (healing, energy boost)

Break open the tea bags into a pot. Coarsely chop the radish greens and add them and the thyme to the same pot. Cover with the olive and almond oils and simmer over low heat until you can smell the herbs in the air. Remove from heat and allow the mixture to cool. Strain the oil into a bottle and charge the oil using the same visualization as in the spring incense instructions.

Powders

Most powders are meant to be used externally, either sprinkled on the ground where needed or used to encircle candles for added power. This powder can be utilized for those purposes as well but is also completely edible (barring any allergy, of course) and can be used as a seasoning, instilling a bit of food magic into an otherwise ordinary meal.

SPRING ZING HERB POWDER

2 teaspoons basil

2 teaspoons oregano

1 teaspoon thyme

1 teaspoon sage

1 teaspoon rosemary

Each of the herbs in this recipe can be used for multiple purposes: love, money, luck, purification, and protection, so the powder makes a great all-purpose magical item. To make: grind the rosemary into as fine a powder as possible, preferably in a coffee grinder. Powder the remaining herbs and add them to the rosemary, stirring to combine. Charge the mixture with pure white light and bottle for use.

POWDER SPELL

As a fast method of magically empowering your food to help reach a goal, a small amount of this powder can be poured into your hand and charged for whatever purpose you choose.

Using the Spring Zing Herb Powder

Visualize the magical goal and say this spell to direct the charge.

To bring forth [state intention], this my spell,
savory herbs and Witch's power;
infused with intention; serve me well,
the magic unleashed, to grow and flower.

Sprinkle the herbs into the food and then the food can be eaten to bring the magic within so that it will begin to have an effect.

Charms

In the spring, resurgence occurs in the natural world; the plants, animals, and birds are more active. In my family, we have always left food out for the birds. Birdseed, dried meal worms (yuck), grains, dried fruit, and so forth. I have always felt that since life can be so unpredictable, it is a person's duty to lend a little stability, help, and comfort when possible. The nature of physical existence is tilted toward decline which in my opinion makes nurturing growth and preservation a powerful spiritual action. Additionally, in magic it is a great act of balance to offer something in return for asking something; it honors the balance and energy exchange. This charm serves both purposes. These ornaments are not only magical talismans that can foster abundance, protection, and improved luck, but they also feed the local birds and honor this phase of nature's cycle.

MAGICAL BIRDSEED ORNAMENTS

Pot

Skewer

Biscuit cutter (or cookie cutters)

Natural twine

Aluminum foil

Cookie sheet

½ cup water

¾ cup flour (abundance)

2½ teaspoons gelatin (binding)

3 tablespoons corn syrup (luck, protection)

1 cup dried cracked corn (luck, protection)

1 cup sunflower seeds, hulled (luck, strength)

1 cup millet (money, luck)

1 cup peanut chips (money, grounding)

A few notes on ingredients: If you have a peanut allergy, an additional cup of sunflower seeds can be used in place of the peanut pieces; cracked corn is usually in the pet food section with birdseed, but unpopped popcorn can be cracked with a mallet to give the same results; millet is harder to find but usually with the organic grains.

To begin, combine the sunflower seeds, cracked corn, peanuts, and millet to create the birdseed mix. Prepare the biscuit cutter by spraying it with cooking spray. Pour the water and corn syrup into a pot and bring to a boil. Lower the heat and then add the gelatin, whisking it in just until dissolved. Remove from heat. In a heatproof mixing bowl combine the syrup mixture with the flour, stirring until well-blended like a thick batter. Add the seed mix into the batter and blend it well into a thick, firm mixture.

Press the seed dough flat onto a foil-covered cutting board. Using the prepared biscuit cutter, cut out several ornaments from the dough, placing the cutouts onto a greased cookie sheet. Drive the skewer through the middle of each cutout to create a hole for hanging the ornaments, being careful not to crack them. If they do crack, press them together again. Allow them to cool and harden overnight before stringing them. Pull the twine through the hole and make a loop to hang from a tree or bird feeder. Charge the ornaments with your desire before hanging. Store extra ornaments in the freezer until needed.

Foods

Of all the foods that are appropriate for this time of year—wonderful green salads; early fruits, vegetables, and herbs—the most prominent food attuned to this season, especially in the popular mind, is the egg. Eggs are symbolic of creation, rejuvenation, rebirth, fertility, and the earth. In this time of waxing light and energy, eggs are powerful magical ingredients for renewal.

Springtime Egg Salad

8 hard-boiled eggs, peeled and washed (rejuvenation)

2 tablespoons celery, chopped (mental clarity)

2 tablespoons onions, chopped (cleansing)

½ cup fat-free or regular mayonnaise (success)

2 teaspoons mustard (purification)

In a bowl, chop the eggs and add the remaining ingredients. Stir to combine and charge the salad with the intention that "this salad shall bring cleansing, renewal, and success to all who consume it, according to free will and for the good of all." Serve immediately or chill until needed.

Bath Salts

This bath salt recipe uses the oil made earlier but combines it with the energy of fresh lemon thereby making the resulting blend perfect for cleansings, healing, and renewal.

Herb-Citrus Bath Salt

2 teaspoons Spring Equinox oil

½ teaspoon lemon juice

1½ cups sea salt

¾ cup Epsom salt

¼ cup baking soda

Mason jar

Combine the salt, baking soda, and Epsom salt. Add the oil and lemon juice, stirring to combine. Hold your hands over the mixture and charge it with your desire. Put salts in the jar and store in a cool dry place.

Witch Bottles

Herb-infused vinegars can add a wonderful decorative element to a kitchen and for us magically-minded folks can also provide a powerful force of spiritual energy, discreetly hidden in plain view. Combining a few key herbs, some simple vinegar, and a few other ingredients with a bit of magical intent into a decorative bottle can create an effective witch bottle that offers protection to the home.

HERB VINEGAR PROTECTION BOTTLE

1 sprig fresh dill (protection)

1 sprig fresh rosemary (protection)

1 sprig fresh oregano or marjoram (protection)

1 sprig fresh sage (protection)

White vinegar

Decorative bottle with tight-fitting lid or cork

White candle (optional)

Bleach

6 cups water

Gather the herbs together and choose the best-looking sprigs. In a bowl, add the water and 1 teaspoon of bleach. Submerge the herbs into the bleach water for a moment and then rinse in clean cool water. Dry the herbs on a kitchen towel. Charge each herb with the intent for protection. Charge the bottle of vinegar with the intentions of protection and of banishing incorrect forces. Clean the bottle thoroughly and slide the herb sprigs into it. Pour in the vinegar just under where the top will be. Close the bottle and if desired, light the white candle and drip wax over the top of the bottle to completely block out air and also to form a magical seal. Display wherever you wish but one word of caution; though this is made with culinary ingredients, this vinegar should not be consumed by anyone. The addition of bleach into the mix is to prevent bacterial spoilage but makes the vinegar unsuitable for food.

Spring Cleaning

Spring cleaning is a term that has become a cliché but in truth, making sure that not only our spiritual lives are in good order but also our everyday physical lives, makes solid sense as we prepare to move into the most active time of the year. Minimizing potential setbacks now gives us stronger momentum to achieve greater ends; proper preparation being such a major part of any success. After you have done any "mundane" regular cleaning, a magical touch can be added by blessing and cleansing what has been cleaned so that the item is renewed not only practically but also spiritually. To clean objects (that are not fragile or easily damaged), you can use magically charged cleaning solutions designed for purification such as the following mixture.

Spring Cleaner

3 bay leaves (purification)

2 chamomile tea bags (peace)

1 tablespoon fennel (purification)

2 peppermint tea bags (purification)

1 tablespoon rosemary (purification, protection)

1 tablespoon sage (purification, protection)

1 tablespoon thyme (purification)

2 cups water (purification)

2 cups white vinegar (purification, banishing)

Pour the water in the pot. Leave the teas in their bags and add them to the pot of water along with the rest of the herbs. On low, heat the herbs and water to a steady simmer until it just begins to boil. Remove from heat and allow the water to cool completely. Strain the herbs out of the water as thoroughly as possible and pour the water into a bottle. Add the vinegar to the bottle and stir the mixture. Charge it with your desire for purification and put on the lid. Use as needed.

To use: this liquid can be added to cleaning water to wash floors or used in a mister bottle to clean glass or counter tops or poured into a bowl in which to dunk or soak small objects.

Holiday: Vernal Equinox

As the shift occurs where the sun is directly over the equator, the hours of day and night become nearly equal and the energies of the planet both light and dark achieve a momentary balance. Equinoxes are so significant in that the whole globe shares in a similar energy at the same time. For the solstices, one half is experiencing the peak of energy while the opposite half must experience the nadir to compensate. Since both the vernal and autumnal equinoxes are both essentially the same astronomical phenomena, for the moment of equinox at least, the world falls into balance. For the vernal equinox, what follows is of course the waxing time of light, so this holiday is not only celebrated for its theme of balance but also as a doorway into the time of growth and increase.

Ritual

To celebrate and acknowledge this terrestrial event, I like to use the eight-spoked wheel symbol to represent the totality of sabbats but I also prefer to make it out of edible ingredients for use in the ritual. I use peanut butter but if an allergy is a concern, it can be substituted with another nut butter or even hummus.

DRAWING IN THE WAXING LIGHT

Peanut butter (or substitute)

Dried apricots (love)

Sunflower seed kernels (fertility, strength)

Plate

Spoon

Green Spring incense (optional)

Incense burner (optional)

Incense charcoal (optional)

Spring Equinox oil

Bowl of ice

Large red candle

Green or white tablecloth

2 white candles

Prior to the ritual, prepare the wheel symbol. On the plate, spread a layer of peanut butter across it so the surface is completely covered. Arrange the sunflower seeds over the peanut butter in two lines so that they make a **+** (a plus sign) then make two more lines forming an X through the plus sign so that eight lines are shown. Use the dried apricots to make a circle around the edge of the plate, encompassing the lines. Place a single dried apricot directly in the center where the lines meet. Refrigerate the wheel until needed.

Create an altar by covering a table or open countertop with the green or white cloth. Set the wheel plate in the center of the altar with the bowl of ice touching it on the left and the red candle (unlit) touching it on the right. Place one white candle in the back of the altar on the left and one on the right; these are the altar candles. Put the incense burner between them, if using. Before the ritual, take a cleansing bath or shower and meditate on the idea of balance; the idea that light and dark can be in harmonious equality and that they may be different expressions of the same reality, essential variances of an underlying essence.

To begin the ritual, light the altar candles and the incense charcoal. When the charcoal is glowing, add the incense. Facing north call out, "Bright green earth warmed and renewed, draw into this space to charge it with power" in order to invoke the earth energies. Turn to face east and say, "Light cool air, flow in from afar, draw into this space to charge it with power" to invoke the power of air. Turn to face the south and say, "Power of revitalizing heat, draw into this space to charge it with power" in order to invoke the power of fire. Turn to face the west and say, "Waters of life, quench and restore, draw into this space to charge it with power" to invoke the power of water.

Facing north once more, place your hands over the wheel plate and say, "Into this wheel, elements combine: earth, air, fire, and water; equal and balanced, merged and entwined, charging this symbol with your power." Visualize the elements coming together into the wheel plate, vitalizing the food with their energies. When you feel ready, light the red candle. While focusing on the bowl of ice, wheel plate, and red candle say:

> *Through the icy winter the earth has emerged*
> *and into the light we begin to go;*
> *the elemental forces are now waxing, we partake*
> *of each to magically grow.*
> *The light has begun to meet the dark and soon*
> *shall overtake it in power;*
> *the earth is warmed by heat of the sun and seeds*
> *will sprout, grow, bloom, and flower.*

Eat some of the wheel to receive the energy of the equinox. If you wish to call any deities to share in your celebration, this is the ideal time to do so. Any magic you would like to work can also be done at this time. Afterward when you are ready to end the rite, thank any deities called and then release the elements by turning to the west, south, east, and north and saying, "Power of (name element), thank you for adding your power to my rite, go in peace and blessed be." Extinguish the candles and the incense and leave any leftover portion of the wheel outdoors as an offering to the wildlife.

Witchy Ways

Since the hard-boiled egg is a staple food and symbol of this time of the year, it may be helpful to look at how to properly cook them. If done right, hard-boiled eggs can turn out perfectly cooked (no runny middles) and easy to peel almost every time. Otherwise, the peel can stick and take most of the egg white with it when removed. The first step is to choose the freshest eggs possible. For practical purposes, this means to wait to buy eggs until a day or two before you plan on using them.

When it comes to the actual cooking, place the eggs in a pot first and then add cool water to the pot. Add an additional inch or so of water above the eggs, so that they are more than covered. Heat the pot over medium heat, uncovered. When the water begins to boil, remove the pot from heat and cover. Allow the pot to sit for 15 minutes to complete the cooking process. Don't lift the lid beforehand or much of the heat will escape. Using a slotted spoon, scoop out the eggs and transfer them to a colander. Run cold water over them to cool them and stop their cooking. Transfer the eggs to a cloth or paper towel to dry before serving (or coloring). Happy spring!

Springtime Shopping List

- Almond oil
- Apricots, dried
- Baking soda
- Basil
- Bay leaves
- Bleach
- Biscuit cutter (or cookie cutter)
- Bottle (with lid or cork)
- Candles (white and red)
- Celery
- Chamomile tea
- Corn syrup
- Corn, cracked
- Dill
- Eggs
- Epsom salts
- Fennel
- Flour
- Gelatin (plain)
- Ginger

- Lemon juice
- Marjoram
- Mason jars
- Mayonnaise (fat-free or regular)
- Millet
- Mustard
- Olive oil
- Onions
- Oranges
- Oregano
- Peanut butter (or substitute)
- Peanut chips
- Peppermint tea
- Plate
- Pot
- Radish greens
- Rosemary
- Sage
- Sea salt
- Skewer
- Spoon

- Sugar (or honey or stevia sweetener)
- Sunflower seeds
- Tablecloth (green or white)
- Tarragon
- Tea (Earl Grey)
- Thyme
- Twine (natural)
- Vinegar (white)

CHAPTER 8

The Eve of May

As the year moves deeper toward the light, we reach the threshold. May Day begins the light half of the year. It is the counterpart to Samhain at the end of October, the doorway into the dark half of the year. There are varying sacred associations to this time of year with many seeing the month of May as a sacred time. The sabbat of Beltane, as the equivalent of Samhain, is a magical day when the doors to the Otherworld are said to open and spirits and faeries are said to be roaming freely about the land. Witch High Priestess Laurie Cabot writes: "On Beltane, Witches celebrate the great fruitfulness of the earth." [8] Australian Witch and High Priestess Ly De Angeles writes in her wonderful book, *When I See the Wild God*: "This season celebrates the

---

8   Laurie Cabot, *Celebrate the Earth* (New York: Delta, 1994), 141.

fair folk and all the high kings and all the high queens from the Dagda to Artu, from Morrigan and Danu to the Ladies of the Lake."[9] Her book gives beautiful insight into how the sabbats are celebrated in the Southern Hemisphere where Beltane occurs in October. No matter where in the world we celebrate it, Beltane and the sacred month that follows open us to the fullness of the bright summer half of the year.

Building Momentum

Since this time begins the upsurge in heat, light, and growth, it is a great time to begin work on magic designed for long-term goals and success. As the power of the earth and sun increase in strength, so too can the results of your growth-related magic. To begin a working for a long-term goal on Beltane, this spell can be of assistance. To work toward accomplishing a goal over the next five months or so (until the autumnal equinox), this spell can be a beginning point. This magic releases your intention and subsequent magic (found in later chapters) can bolster it along the way, until the intention has manifested. Such goals as ideal employment, purchasing a home or a new car, or having a child are appropriate for this type of spellwork.

Essentials of Life Spell
1 green candle (growth, abundance)

---

9   Ly De Angeles, *When I See the Wild God* (St. Paul, MN: Llewellyn Publications, 2004), 149.

1 empty spice bottle with lid

1 cup salt (blessing)

1 cup milk (nourishment)

1 cup water (sustenance)

Paper and pen

Cauldron or heatproof bowl

Place the green candle in the center of a table. To the north of the candle, set the salt. To the east of the candle, set the cup of milk. To the south of the candle, set the cauldron, and to the west, set the cup of water. For vegans or those who avoid dairy, almond, soy, or rice milk are appropriate substitutes. Write your goal on the paper and channel all of your resolve into the paper; see yourself achieving it and feeling that joy.

Light the green candle. Focus on the candle's flame and sense how essential it is to existence. Without the heat and light of the fire element, life would not be possible. Using your dominant hand, touch your thumb to the water and bring it to your lips. Reflect on how essential this liquid is to existence. Most of this planet is composed of water, most of our body is composed of water, and without drinking water, we could not live. Touch the same thumb to the salt and taste it. Ponder how essential this substance is to life. Did you know that salt does not conduct electricity and water does not conduct electricity but saltwater does? The salt molecules move through the fluid of the water making transference possible. Salt (sodium) is a vital nutrient in our bodies (admittedly, too much can be harmful) helping to regulate fluid balance and nerve transmissions among other functions.[10] Salt is also a preservative and in the past before refrigeration was possible, salt was immeasurably important in food preservation. Not only this, but salt is seen as being symbolic of the earth overall, its mineral nature representing all the land. Finally, touch your thumb to the milk and bring it to your lips. Reflect on how vital milk is to our lives. While not every living thing drinks milk—in fact, only mammals do—it is still symbolic of basic sustenance from the mother; that essential life-sustaining nutrition every form of life needs to survive. Though it could easily be argued that milk is only essential in infancy for mammals of any type, that does not diminish its significance or miraculous nature. Fire, water, salt, and milk, together here as four vital and sacred things part of nearly every home.

Once you have connected to these substances, touch a corner of the paper to each one: water, salt, milk, flame, allowing the fire to engulf the paper, then drop it into the cauldron to burn to ashes. As the paper burns say,

> *As I honor the essentials of life, so do I ask them to sustain me,*

----

10   Harvard Health Publications, *Salt and Your Health, Part 1: The Sodium Connection*, (health.harvard.edu/newsletter_article/salt-and-your -health, 2016).

*I pledge to keep my stocks refilled, never letting them
run bare;
Let this form a strong foundation to help attain the
goals I seek,
Then with abundance newly built, from my bounty I
happily share.*

Once the ashes have cooled, mix in a tiny, tiny pinch of salt along with the milk and water. Pour this mixture out, ideally on the threshold of your home or in a flowerpot near the front of your home to release the energy. Pour the remaining salt in the spice bottle and reserve for future work on this goal. Always keep a supply of milk, salt, water, and a source of flame in your home while working this magic.

HOLIDAY: Beltane

This holiday connects us to the active side of life; that primal force of generation and renewal. Its symbols are frequently related to archetypal sexual union: the maypole implanted into the earth; the fire kindled within the cauldron; the athame lowered into the chalice; all not only standing for that transformative union of sex, but also much deeper spiritual truths. The maypole for example is not only symbolic of the penis but also representative of the tree of life; the sacred world tree whose branches reach into the stars, trunk in our plane, and roots that stretch down into the underworld. The maypole then becomes an axis that can channel spiritual power and assist us in communicating with otherworld beings and forces.[11] The cauldron not only symbolizes the womb containing the fires of life, it also represents the goddess and her eternal nature and influence. To kindle a fire within the cauldron is to offer acknowledgement of her sacred power.

Not only used on Beltane but also a frequent feature of most rituals, the symbolism of the athame lowered into the cup is strong. The blade represents the Witch's will-power—the hilt stands for our intent and the point of the double-edged blade is the meeting place for both the seen and unseen. The chalice of course symbolizes life itself; the vessel of creation holding its creation, often represented by wine. The wine (or other beverage) in the cup repre-sents the current incarnation of forever, the molecules of the liquid being comprised of atoms that have always been in some form a part of the universe. When the blade is lowered into the cup to charge and bless the wine, it is a magical consecration; the will and intent of the Witch combining with the powers of creation and eternity. To partake of this blessed liquid is to commune with the sa-cred forces of nature.

Whichever ritual acts we choose to perform during sabbat celebrations, we should be aware of their higher meaning. It is not "wrong" to focus on the more sexual-ity or fertility-based aspects of the Beltane holiday, but

---

11   Gwyn, *Light From the Shadows: Modern Traditional Witchcraft* (Taunton, UK: Capall Bann, 1999), 124.

to mistake the physical expressions of these factors as the only relevant elements would, in my opinion, be missing out on their deeper significance. All aspects can be celebrated according to free will and desire. There are so many options to create a rich and rewarding holiday experience that touch not only the physical realm but also into the otherworld. The essence of magic is to create change and any act of magic can be a spiritual act if done with proper reverence.

Simmering Potpourris

As the season warms and we are able to increase our activities, chaos can sometimes become the norm. If we have to coordinate schedules, activities, and obligations, tensions can build. It helps to have magical methods for restoring a peaceful environment if things get hectic. It is also a good idea to use the following recipe periodically to avoid tension in the first place.

PEACEFUL HOME POTPOURRI

2 cups apple juice (love, healing)

1 teaspoon vanilla extract (energy)

1 teaspoon almond extract (prosperity)

2 tablespoons cinnamon (spirituality)

1 teaspoon cloves (love, banishing)

Stir the spices and extracts into the apple juice, charge with intent, and simmer the mixture on the stove to encourage calm and peace. Add water or more apple juice as needed if the levels get too low in the pot.

Brews

This brew captures a similar essence as the more traditional May wine, but without the alcohol or the woodruff herb, which is not readily available at most supermarkets (though sometimes for sale at a health food store). This drink can be used as a libation, a festive beverage for two, or the recipe can be doubled or tripled and it can be served in a punch bowl.

MAY DAY SPARKLE BREW

1 cup white grape juice (abundance)

1 cup club soda (releasing energy)

½ cup water (purification)

1 teaspoon vanilla extract (love, energy)

1 tablespoon strawberry jam, 100 percent
fruit (love, luck)

½ teaspoon rosemary (purification)

Heat the water in a small pot until it just starts to boil (add a little more water if necessary). Place the rosemary in a heatproof mug, bowl, or pitcher and pour the water over it.

Allow the rosemary infusion to steep until the water has cooled (20 minutes to an hour). Strain out the rosemary and stir in the strawberry jam and vanilla extract. Add the white grape juice, stir again, and charge with your intent. Pour the mixture into cups so that each cup is half full. Add club soda to fill each cup and serve.

Incense

The ingredients of this incense are all in tune with the passionate, high-energy fire of this holiday. They are green, bright, and powerfully magical.

BELTANE POWER INCENSE

1 tablespoon marjoram (all-purpose)

1 tablespoon rosemary (all-purpose)

¼ teaspoon coriander (love, lust, healing)

Combine the herbs in a bowl and grind them together with your fingers or the back of a spoon. You could also use a mortar and pestle to crush and blend the herbs. Charge the mixture to be an incense of Beltane and bottle for use.

Oils

This oil is dual purpose; it is a magical oil for Beltane but also can be used as a spicy cooking oil for frying or basting vegetables or meat.

Beltane Fire Oil

1 cup almond oil (prosperity)

1 tablespoon chili flakes (passion)

1 tablespoon paprika (magical enhancer)

Sprinkle the chili flakes and paprika in a pot and cover with the oil. Warm the oil over low heat just until you can smell it (be careful with this one as the aroma can be irritating). Remove from heat and allow to cool. Charge the oil to be attuned to the holiday, strain, and bottle for use.

Oil Spell

This bit of food magic can be a delightful boost to the sabbat feast. It is a recipe that is vegan, spicy, hearty, and completely in tune with the season. Mushrooms are one of the foods that work well with Beltane and they provide a wonderful magic all their own.

Magical Grilled Mushrooms

1 pound white button mushrooms or preferred
   type (psychic awareness, balance)

Beltane Fire oil

Basting brush

Salt

Skewers

Wash the mushrooms and arrange them on a large plate. Brush them with the Beltane Fire oil and then sprinkle them with salt. If you are using a larger variety of mushroom, such as a portabella, there is no need to skewer, but for the smaller mushrooms, arrange several on each skewer, leaving a little space between each one. Charge the mushrooms to be food that will help to open your awareness to the energy of this holiday. On a preheated grill, place the mushrooms in the center area and cook them 5 to 8 minutes, flipping and basting them with the oil halfway between. Remove from the grill and serve.

Powders

This powder is a lively blend of green vitality mixed with the strong purifying powers of the onion. It can be used to ring candles for healing magic, dusted across thresholds to guard them from unwelcome influences, or even sprinkled into foods to bring magical healing and purification energies within.

PURIFYING AND HEALING POWDER

2 peppermint tea bags (purification, healing)

1 tablespoon marjoram (healing)

1 tablespoon onion powder (purification, healing, banishing)

Open the tea bags into a bowl and add the marjoram. Break up the leaves with your fingers and add the onion powder. Gently stir to combine and charge the mixture with your intent for purification and healing and bottle for use.

Powder Spell
Green Healing Candle Spell

1 green candle

Purifying and Healing powder

Olive oil

Paper

Pen

Plate

Cauldron or heatproof bowl

Write down what you wish to be healed. Fold the paper in half and in half again.

If you want something restored like a wound or broken bone, fold the paper toward you. If you want the healing to take something away, such as a wart or an illness, fold the paper away from you. Set the paper on the working table. Anoint the candle with the olive oil, from the top to the middle and from the bottom up to the middle. Sprinkle the healing powder on a plate and roll the candle in the powder being careful to avoid getting the powder stuck to the wick. Set the candle on the table near the paper.

Focusing very strongly on your magical goal, light the green candle and gaze at its flame. Once the flame is burning steady, pick up the paper, light it from the candle and as you drop it in the cauldron, say the spell.

> *Through healing magic and candle's flame,*
> *restore the body to glowing health;*
> *what once was whole, return again,*
> *let strength and vigor be freely felt.*

Allow the paper to burn out completely and once the ashes have cooled (pour water on them if unsure) bury them outdoors or in a flowerpot.

Charms

With this season being the light counterpart to the Samhain season, mischievous unseen beings could be out to stir up trouble. In this case, it never hurts to have some magical protection. Even without otherworldly creatures, mundane mischief is also best deflected or blocked. This charm bag is not only protective in nature, but also lends the added touch of increased psychic awareness so that danger can be more easily avoided.

HEIGHTENED PROTECTION AMULET

1 teaspoon dried mushrooms (psychic awareness)

¼ teaspoon flax seeds (protection)

1 teaspoon oregano (protection)

1 teaspoon radish greens, dried (protection)

Cheesecloth

Red thread or natural twine

Layer two squares of cheesecloth. In the middle of the square, place the mushrooms, flax seeds, oregano, and radish greens. Hold your hands over the herbs and charge them with the intent that they shall form a powerful bundle to protect from harm and alert when danger is near. Gather the corners of the cheesecloth and twist around the bundle, capturing the herbs within. Wind the red thread around the bundle several times and secure it with three knots. Once more, focus on the magical goal and say the spell.

> *Root and seed and leaf combine,*
> *with fairy cap to bolster the charm;*
> *magic bundle, bound with red twine,*
> *and knotted thrice to protect from harm.*

This charm can be kept on your person or in your home or car as desired.

Foods

Oats are one of the ritually appropriate food staples of this time of year. They are magically aligned with abundance and this energy is perfect for Beltane. Dairy products such as butter or cheese are appropriate as well since these items are symbolic of transformation. Though they are more prominently featured in their hard-cooked form at the spring equinox, eggs are another magical ingredient that is appropriate at this time. They are symbolic of fertility and rejuvenation, both important themes of Beltane. Potatoes are another fine food for this time of year. Their magic relates to healing and moon work. A fine meal for either a Beltane breakfast or as part of the ritual feast that combines all of these foods is a special frittata with oat bread toast.

Sunny May Day Frittata

1 yellow onion (protection, healing)

1 teaspoon garlic, minced (protection, healing)

3 potatoes, sliced ¼-inch thick (healing)

6 eggs (rejuvenation)

¼ cup milk (healing, protection)

2 tablespoons butter (transformation)

1 teaspoon oregano, crumbled
   (protection, healing)

Pinch paprika (magical booster)

Pinch curry powder (purification)

Salt and pepper to taste

¾ cup cheese, sharp cheddar or pepper
   jack recommended (transformation)

Frying pan that is oven-safe

Preheat the broiler in the oven. Charge the ingredients separately with your intent. After the potatoes are sliced, cook them in lightly salted boiling water until they are fork-tender, about 5 to 10 minutes. Drain the potatoes and reserve. Chop the onion and add it and the garlic to a frying pan along with the butter. Sauté until the onion is translucent, 3 to 5 minutes. To the pan, add the sliced potatoes and the herbs and spices. Stir gently to combine. Scramble the eggs in a bowl with the milk and salt and pepper to taste. Pour them over the potatoes and onions in the pan. Lightly stir them with a spatula so that they set in "large curds" as they cook for 2 to 3 minutes. Sprinkle ½ cup of the cheese evenly over the surface of the frittata and press it in lightly with a fork or spatula. Add the remaining cheese over the top and set the pan in the oven. Broil until the eggs are puffed and set and the cheese begins to brown in spots, approximately 2 minutes. Remove from the oven and let stand for 10 to 15 minutes before slicing. Serve with whole grain oat bread, toasted and topped with butter.

Bath Salts

This lively formula creates a purifying bath salt that helps align your energies with that of Beltane. It is great for a pre-ritual bath.

Bright Fire Bath Salt

1½ cups sea salt

¾ cup Epsom salt

¼ cup baking soda

½ ounce Beltane Fire oil (prosperity, passion)

3 drops mint extract (healing, purification)

Mix the baking soda, sea salt, and Epsom salt together in a bowl. Stir in the magical oil and the drops of mint extract. Charge the mixture with your intent that it help to connect you to the energy of the sabbat. Bottle for use. A word of caution: do not use this mixture if you have a cut or broken skin as it can be irritating (with the salt, mint, and spices in the Beltane oil); keep away from your eyes.

Beltane Special Formula

Beginning on Beltane Eve and continuing throughout the month that follows, faeries and otherworldly spirits are said to be roaming freely across the land. Though in modern times there is a much more benevolent view of faery beings, many legends exist of fearsome or trouble-making fey that are best warded off. In the ancient past, this was considered much more of a problem than it is today, and there were a great many formulas and procedures designed to keep harmful faeries at bay. Many strong plants and herbs were used to lend their protective magic around the home and also for pets and cattle to safeguard their lives and health.

One of the prized plants for protection against the supernatural is the fennel. Though there are several varieties, both wild and cultivated, all have protective qualities. In the past, fennel was hung above doorways to prevent evil from entering and an ointment was created from fennel that was used to anoint the udders of cattle in order to protect their milk from being stolen or soured by mischievous faeries.[12]

FAERY PROTECTION OINTMENT

1 fennel bulb, with fronds (protection)

1 cup plus 3 tablespoons shortening (neutral base)

1 teaspoon water

Mason jar

Chop the fennel bulb, fronds and all, and place it in a frying pan along with the 3 tablespoons of shortening (vegetable shortening is the best choice for this recipe especially if you will be using the ointment on people or animals). Over medium heat, sauté the fennel until it just begins to caramelize, about 5 minutes. Add a teaspoon of water to the pan to allow it to steam for 1 minute more then remove from heat. Stir in the remaining cup of shortening and allow it to melt completely. Pour the mixture into a mason jar. If you would like a smoother ointment, you can

---

12   Vivian A. Rich, *Cursing the Basil and Other Folklore from the Garden* (Victoria, BC: Touchwood Editions, 2010), 142–143.

strain it through a metal sieve as you pour. Let the ointment cool completely and charge with your intent.

Using the Faery Protection Ointment

This salve can be used in much the same way that you would a magical oil; to anoint the wrists, third eye, and back of the neck for protection, to lightly anoint a pet on the back of the neck (where they can't lick it off), or to touch the inside of doorways or objects to offer them protection. It can also be applied lightly to the front and rear bumper of a car to lends its power. Store the ointment in the refrigerator to avoid it turning rancid. The ointment should last about one month. More information and recipes relating to faeries can be found in upcoming chapters.

Ritual

As the momentum of energy increases and the tide turns toward the more active half of the year, the sabbat of Beltane is acknowledged as a door—the gateway from the cold, dark portion of nature's cycle to emerge renewed into the light. This holiday is a joyous celebration of life and abundance. In this ritual are four main themes that will be addressed: waking up the land, connecting to the power of the otherworld and the earth, "turning the wheel" with a modern version of lighting the Bel-fire, and partaking of the energy of the season so it may empower you.

Three Realms Beltane Rite

Broom, new and unused with wooden handle

Dustpan

9 green candles

Athame

Cup

Cauldron or heatproof bowl

Large planter pot with potting soil (optional)

This is a ritual that can be done outdoors and if that is possible, so much the better. If the rite is conducted outdoors, a small table should be set up for an altar, preferably on open land. Just north of the altar, it should be possible to drive the handle of the broom into the earth, deep enough for it to be free standing. Dig a hole in the ground and then refill it with the same dirt if needed. The choice of buying a large planter urn and potting soil to act as the vessel to hold the broom is another good option. Prior to the rite, if you have a garden, you can walk through it holding the broom so that its bristles brush just above the plants and visualize this as blessing the plants with growth and health and protecting them from harm.

On the altar, place the cauldron in the center with one candle within and the remaining candles surrounding it: one at each of the direction points of north, east, south, west, and one in between each direction. These candles are standing in place of the Beltane fire. As a bonfire, in some traditions nine different woods are used: birch, oak, hazel, rowan, hawthorn, willow, fir, apple, and vine. However I think candles will suffice as these woods are not readily available at the supermarket. Green is an ideal color for the Beltane candles, but if you wish to represent the nine different woods, nine different colored candles can be used, if that many colors could be found. Set the cup, filled with red wine (or grape juice), on the left of the altar and the athame on the right.

If the ritual is to take place indoors, the broom can simply be leaned against the altar so that it stands (mostly) upright or the planter pot can be carefully brought indoors. Either way, sweep the area thoroughly with the broom. Normally when using a broom in magic, this is done in a symbolic sense, but in this case, literal cleaning is required. Sweep the floor (or ground) and gather up any debris into a dustpan and throw it out the back door, away from your home. If outdoors, simply throw the dirt away at the farthest point in your yard. Physically removing the old dust or dirt serves to cleanse and awaken your personal space and in turn signals the land to your presence and intention.

After the sweeping, use the broom to encircle yourself within the working area in a circle of energy, using the broom as a magical staff. Drive the handle of the broom into the ground so that it stands straight up with the bristles pointed toward the sky. If indoors, the broom may have to be placed bristle-side down against the table so that it won't tip over, which is fine. As you set the broom, visualize that it is sending out beacons of light above and below, to the heavens and down to the underworld, connecting all three realms. This reaching out to the otherworld in both directions creates a channel through which we can receive spiritual blessings and also send our magic outward with greater ease. To proclaim this work, as you place the broom say:

> *Witch's broom of magic might,*
> *stretch your energy above and below;*
> *grant me access to heavenly light,*
> *and deep earth power help bestow.*

Light the eight candles around the cauldron proclaiming, "Here I light the bright fire of Beltane to warm the land and turn the wheel." Light the ninth candle in the cauldron and say, "May the season be green and the earth be fertile, restoring the balance, damages heal." If you are going to call upon deities, this is the ideal time to do so. Offerings can be given, thanks and prayers be spoken, and any spells—particularly those for protection—can be worked as well.

To draw in the energy of the sabbat and the blessing of the deities, the wine can now be consecrated. Holding the cup in your weak hand and the athame in your strong hand, lower the tip of the knife into the wine, visualize white light pouring into the liquid and say:

Vessel of creation, elixir of life,
union of spirit and flesh combine;
liquid charged through cup and knife,
pierce the veil and bless the wine.

Set down the athame, hold the cup up with both hands in salute, and drink of the wine to share in the communion of all.

Thank any deities, faeries, or elementals you have called and extinguish all of the candles except for the one in the cauldron. Focus your mind on the broom and visualize that its energies are being drawn back from the upper and lower realms, restoring the broom to its ordinary state. As you visualize proclaim, "Its energy spent, the power withdraws, to be unleashed again when there is need. With thanks and honor to spirit kin, the gates are closed and blessed be." Pull the broom from its post and use it to "cut" open the circle. Return to the cauldron and before you extinguish the candle say, "With thanks and love this sabbat is released, the power is claimed and magic set free." Feasting and relaxation follows.

Witchy Ways

Though the maypole is easily recognized as a facet of this holiday in some regions, another important symbol of Beltane is the maybush, a decorated bush that symbolizes the joy and fertility of the holiday. It's similar to a Christmas tree though it is usually decorated with colorful eggshells, ribbons, small fruits, and little trinkets. If you have a small outdoor bush or a sturdy indoor plant, this is a fun and traditional decoration to try. Just decorate it how you see fit in honor of the sabbat.

Beltane Shopping List

- Almond extract

- Almond oil

- Apple juice

- Baking soda

- Basting brush

- Broom

- Butter

- Candles, green

- Cheese

- Cheesecloth

- Chili flakes

- Cinnamon

- Cloves

- Club soda

- Coriander

- Curry powder

- Dustpan

- Eggs
- Epsom salt
- Fennel
- Flax seeds
- Frying pan (oven safe)
- Garlic
- Grape juice, white
- Marjoram
- Mason jars
- Milk
- Mint
- Mint extract
- Mushrooms, fresh and dried
- Oat bread
- Olive oil
- Onion powder
- Onion, yellow
- Oregano
- Paper
- Paprika
- Pen

- Pepper, black
- Peppermint tea
- Plate
- Potatoes
- Radish greens
- Red thread or twine
- Rosemary
- Salt
- Sea salt
- Shortening, vegetable
- Skewers
- Spice bottle, empty
- Strawberry jam, 100 percent fruit
- Vanilla extract
- Wine, red

SECTION 3

SUMMER SURGE

With the light half of the year in full swing, we approach the midpoint of its power. Since the ancient year was divided in two with Beltane initiating the summer half, the time of the solstice occurs not at the beginning of this phase but rather at the peak of power in the center. Using the two-season model of the year puts this solstice celebration as a midsummer feast, which is what it is frequently named. Some other names for this holiday include: Litha, Alban Hefin, and Mean Samhraidh, to name a few.

CHAPTER 9

Power of Summer

Summer is the height of power for both heat and light. What was sprouted in spring comes into full strength during the summer. We reach the zenith of solar power where we experience the longest day of the year, but this also means that the light will begin to recede after this day. This duality of surging power and subsequent recession marks the solstice another liminal (transitional, threshold) time with magical implications similar to those of Beltane and Samhain. The summer solstice is a time of strong otherworldly power and influence when the faeries and nature spirits can roam freely about the land. We may choose to communicate with the benevolent fey and ward off the power of those more antagonistic faery folk.

Faeries and Enchantment

The perception people have of the faery folk varies greatly depending on region of the world or cultural context. While some believe the faery are an "elder race" that occupied the earth before the dawn of human civilization and eventually moved deeper into their own spiritual realm, others see them as the "soul of nature," the spiritual essences of the living beings of the world. There are other folk beliefs that the faeries are spirits of the dead or even hybrid beings that resulted in mating between human beings and fallen angels. This last viewpoint appears to be heavily influenced by Christian concepts.[13] My own view combines some of these ideas. I think that the idea of the faery being an elder race has merit since humanity has only been on earth for a relatively short time. If they are an elder and magical race, it would also stand to reason that they have an intrinsic connection to their surroundings which would support their nature spirit status as well. Personally, I am pretty convinced that the spirits of departed humans are not of the same type as those of the faery although there may be some crossover and they can certainly have a similar effect on our world. Regardless of what their unique and amazing origins may be, they have been a part of the lore and Craft of the Witch for generations.

---

13   Gwyn, *Light from the Shadows: Modern Traditional Witchcraft* (Taunton, UK: Capall Bann, 1999), 132–137.

So many methods of contact and collaboration and conversely warding and protection toward the faery folk have developed over the centuries, and many of these customs use ingredients which can now be found in our modern supermarkets. One of the most basic ways to gain the favor of nature faeries is to honor the plant kingdom. Grow a small garden or even just one herb or vegetable in a flowerpot. Carefully tend to it as a way to respect their realm. Another method for gaining their favor is to leave a libation out in nature such as a bowl of fresh water, cream, or the following brew.

Brews

While this recipe is intended to be a gift left for the faery realm, it actually could be consumed by a person to help them sleep.

FAERY LIBATION BREW

1 cup milk (healing)

2 teaspoons honey (healing, blessing)

1 teaspoon unsalted butter
   (transformation, blessing)

Warm the milk in a pot over medium heat just until it starts to foam up then quickly remove from heat. Stir in the honey and the butter and pour into a bowl or cup that can stay outdoors. Allow the brew to cool and the flavors to mingle before using it.

Brew Spell

This simple spell can be used to begin or maintain contact with the faery beings in your general area.

Befriending the Local Faeries

Bowl

Faery Libation brew

Charge the brew with your desire that it will bless those that consume it and take to an outdoor location that you feel has a faery presence to it. Anywhere can be chosen; your own garden, the base of a tree, or some lonely wild place in the woods, wherever you would like to attempt contact. Of course, if a distant location is chosen the milk will have to be bottled for transport and then poured into the cup or bowl.

As you set the bowl in place, call out to the faeries with a clear message if intent such as, "Faery folk of blessed land, I leave an offering of honeyed cream; pleasant favor I ask you grant, to build a link between your realm and me; accept this gift as freely bestowed and helping a magical bond to grow." Leave the bowl without looking back. Three days later, return to collect the bowl. The bowl may be empty or there might still be some of the milk left in it. Either way, if you feel welcomed in the area, further offerings can be left and spells can be worked in that area which can become your own little "enchanted land." If however, you feel uneasy or rejected, it is best to break off attempts at contact in this area.

Incense

The smoke of incense can help to carry the message of your intent into the otherworld. The most important factor of incense is the energy of the ingredients. Though ideally the smoke would be pleasant, this is not always the case nor is an agreeable aroma necessary (or especially important) in transmitting magical intent. This incense is formulated to assist in communication with the faery realm.

FAERY CALL INCENSE

3 tablespoons thyme (healing, faery magic)

1 teaspoon apple peel, dried (love, faery magic)

1 hazelnut, shelled and crushed (wisdom)

Grate or finely mince the skin of an apple and allow it to completely dry. Add to this the thyme and crushed hazelnut. Charge the incense with your intent and bottle for use.

Oils

This formula creates a magical oil suitable for aiding communication with the faery folk which may be roaming nearby.

Faery's Call Oil

1 tablespoon dried apple peel (love, faery magic)

1 teaspoon thyme (healing, energy)

1 teaspoon rosemary (purification, wisdom)

½ teaspoon poppy seeds (moon magic, love)

1 hazelnut, shelled and crushed (wisdom)

1 small fresh mushroom, sliced
   (psychic awareness)

½ cup almond oil (wisdom, communication)

Pour the oil in a pan and add the sliced mushroom. Sauté the mushroom over low heat until it is cooked through. Add the remaining ingredients, stirring to combine, and heat until you can smell the herbs. Remove from heat and allow it to cool before straining, charging, and bottling the oil.

Powders

One of the most popular notions about faeries is that they have the power to grant wishes. In a great many stories, we see the faery princess, leprechaun, or faery godmother granting wonderful wishes, making someone's dream come true. However, waiting for that faery godmother to show up is far too time-consuming, at least for my taste! I prefer to make my own magic. This powder recipe draws upon the energies of the planets and elements to create a special wishing formula that can help achieve nearly any purpose, no pixie dust required.

ALL-PURPOSE WISHING POWDER

1 teaspoon arrowroot (Mars, healing, purification)

1 teaspoon sage (Jupiter, wishing, prosperity)

1 teaspoon cinnamon (Sun, spirituality, success)

1 teaspoon dill (Mercury, love, money)

1 teaspoon lemon zest (Moon, purification, love)

1 teaspoon oat flour (Venus, abundance)

1 teaspoon poppy seeds (Neptune, love, money)

1 teaspoon fresh broccoli (Saturn, strength, empowerment)

1 teaspoon rye flour (Pluto, love, protection)

1 teaspoon lime zest (Uranus, love, healing, purification)

For the broccoli, brush off the little tips of the florets into a bowl, leaving the stalk. This way, you'll have a teaspoon of small granules. They are usually dry enough on their own unless the broccoli is wet. To be sure, you can leave it out to dry overnight. For the lemon and lime zests, let them dry before creating the powder. Grind all of the ingredients together (a coffee grinder works great for this) and empower the powder with the intent that it will help to manifest your desires. Bottle for use.

Charms

Though much of the magic of faery work focuses on contact, there is also a need for protection from those faery beings that are not well disposed to humanity; one simple and effective means of protection against the faery is iron. This charm uses four simple ingredients to create a powerful barrier for your home to keep it safe from harm.

THE IRON SHIELD

Small cast iron pan (protection)

Hydrogen peroxide

Salt (blessing, protection)

Paper towels

Wash and dry the cast iron pan. Apply some of the peroxide to a paper towel and wipe a thin coating on the inside of the pan on the cooking surface. Next, carefully pour a line of salt onto the pan in the shape of a pentagram. Allow the peroxide and salt to dry overnight on the pan and then brush off the salt. Empower the pan with your desire for protection. Bury the pan outside your home in order to protect the area. If burying is not possible, secret it away in a safe place within your home, just make sure it is wrapped in something so that it will not ruin anything with rust.

Foods

This time of year is all about warmth and abundance; the richness of life. One of my favorite parts of summer is the wealth of fresh fruits that become available: nectarines, cherries, berries, melons, plums, and the wonderful peach. Peaches are magical (and delicious) fruits. Botanically related to roses, their magic is concerned with love, fertility, and enchantment. Though any dish made with peaches can help in these areas, as can eating them fresh, in the summer my sweet tooth cries out for fresh baked goods.

This dish, a nice version of the classic peach pie, is centered on faery magic with the addition of honey and butter, two legendary faery foods.

HONEY-BUTTER PEACH PIE

Fresh peaches, 8 small or 5 large (love, fertility, enchantment)

1 tablespoon lemon juice (love, purification)

½ cup sugar (love, purification)

1 teaspoon nutmeg (love, healing)

¼ cup honey (love, faery magic)

2 teaspoons cinnamon (spirituality, love, success)

⅓ cup flour (abundance, fertility)

2 tablespoons butter, diced (transformation, faery magic)

2 prepared pie crusts (abundance, transformation)

Wash and slice the peaches into a bowl (I usually cut them in fourths and then each quarter in half again). Drizzle the lemon juice over the peaches. In a second bowl, combine the sugar, nutmeg, cinnamon and flour. Pour the honey over the peaches and then pour the mixed dry ingredients on top. Stir together gently and then pour this pie filling into one of the crusts and dot the peaches with the bits of butter.

Place the other crust on top, pressing the edges to seal. You can use your thumb to press the dough together on the rim of the pan to make a decorative crust or use the tines of a fork to create a crimped edge. Cut slits on the top of the crust to allow air to escape. Empower the pie with your intent and bake it in a 350° F oven for 50 to 65 minutes, until the peaches are bubbling and the crust is golden brown. Cool before serving; to further empower the magic, this pie can be paired with natural vanilla ice cream.

Witch Bottles

Though that elusive magic pixie dust may be hard to find, we can harness a similar power. This witch bottle is going to create a powerful ground in which to manifest your intentions. We can create our own faery dust mixture and use it to vitalize our magic so that what is placed into the bottle will be charged with magical energy and intention.

Faery Dust Wishing Bottle

1 tablespoon rosemary (all-purpose)

1 tablespoon hazelnuts, crushed (wisdom)

1 tablespoon sage (cleansing)

1 tablespoon sunflower seeds, crushed
   (luck, strength)

1 tablespoon pomegranate seeds, dried (luck)

1 tablespoon walnuts, crushed (healing, strength)

1 cup colored baking sugar, in chosen color

Mason jar or bottle with lid (minimum
   2 cup capacity)

Paper and pen

Place the first six ingredients into a coffee grinder or food processor and grind them into as fine a powder as possible. Do not over-grind or you will end up with some type of nut butter. Just grind them down to a "chunky-style" powder. Pour the powder into a bowl and stir in the baking sugar. If you have trouble finding the sugar, you can use the cake sprinkles sold in those little bottles by the birthday candles. It is basically the same thing as baking sugar and has the same attributes. Charge this with your intention. Write your wish on the piece of paper and roll it up into a scroll. Put the scroll into the bottle and pour the faery dust around it. Seal the bottle and place it where you will see it often but it will not be handled by others.

Summer Faery Shopping List

- Almond oil
- Apples
- Arrowroot
- Broccoli
- Butter
- Cast iron pan
- Cinnamon
- Colored sugar
- Dill
- Flour
- Hazelnuts
- Honey
- Hydrogen peroxide
- Lemons
- Limes
- Mason jar
- Milk
- Mushrooms
- Nutmeg
- Oat flour

- Paper towels
- Pie crusts
- Pomegranates
- Poppy seeds
- Rye flour
- Rosemary
- Sage
- Salt
- Sugar
- Sunflower seeds
- Thyme
- Walnuts

CHAPTER 10

Solstice of Water and Fire

The summer solstice is a funny thing—in the Northern Hemisphere it occurs at the point of shift from the mutable air energy of Gemini to the cardinal water energy of Cancer. This could explain why in many areas summer heat is slow to develop since the vital, nurturing energy of Cancer begins the season of strongest growth but then transfers into the fixed fire sign of Leo which solidifies the intensity of heat. In the Southern Hemisphere however, the summer solstice occurs during the transfer of power from the mutable fire sign of Sagittarius to the cardinal earth sign of Capricorn leading to the fixed air sign of Aquarius at the center of the season which creates a vastly different seasonal dynamic.

In either hemisphere, though the season of summer is primarily associated with the element of fire, each element can make itself known in powerful ways: hurricanes, heavy rains, and turbulent winds, to mudslides and seemingly endless heat waves. Luckily, a lot of the more extreme manifestations of summer's power are irregular occurrences; the bulk of summertime energy is tied to the promotion of growth. Most of the crops grow to their fullest during this phase in time for the harvest in autumn, so even though some of the weather may be harsh (I know that for me, the +100° F heat waves get old fast), the season is still a vital part of the year's cycle.

Magic of the Sea

Despite the dominant awareness of summertime in relation to the land, the sea and its beautiful wonders are also very much a part of the summer season both as a popular vacation destination and as a major component of weather patterns. Even if we can't go to the seashore and touch the warm sand or let the waves crash against our legs, we can still call upon the energy and magical inhabitants of the ocean for use in our magic and to build greater spiritual connection to this mystical realm. Fortunately, there are options for creating these magical calls; channels to draw in the energy and the ingredients to aid in this work can all be found at the supermarket.

Probably the most easily recognizable magical figure linked to the sea is the mermaid. From the nereids, the

Greek sea nymphs; the ancient Irish merrows or liban; the Japanese ningyo; or any of the myriad sea sprites and faeries that make their home deep in the waters of the seas according to legend and folklore, the tales of magical undersea beings are almost universal. Calling to the faeries of the waters is a wonderful way to expand your spirituality, awareness of emotions, ecology, the ocean, and the water element. Beyond these reasons, mermaid energy can help you in magic relating to love, protection during water travel, and divination.

To Call the Mermaid

Mermaids are mystical beings whose energy can come through almost any type of water, saltwater being the strongest form.

Cauldron or black bowl

1 tablespoon grape seed oil (sea magic)

1 tablespoon hazelnut oil (wisdom)

1 blue candle (water element)

Water, lightly salted

On a low table, set the cauldron in the center with water inside it and put the candle far enough behind it so that its light will not be reflected on the water. Light the candle and gaze into the water. Relax your mind and think of the ocean. Try to mentally conjure the sound of the crashing waves, the call of the sea gulls, and the smell of the ocean mist; fill yourself with the energy of the waters. Call to the mermaids. Pour the hazelnut and grape seed oils into the water and visualize that doing so will create a magical watery window into their realm. Communicate with them. Reach out with your emotions and ask that they come to you. When you feel as though contact has been established, you can then ask for their assistance. It is best to try and establish an alliance; a strong working partnership where both sides give and take rather than seeking them as a novelty or magical accessory. Ask what they would like in return for their help and thank them for their presence. Bid them farewell and end the ritual. Extinguish the candle and pour out the water. Clean and dry the cauldron right away so it does not rust.

The Power of the Dragons

Though there are dragons that are aligned with different elements, they are historically associated with fire. Since the more dominant themes of summer are heat and fire, it is these dragon forms I focus on here. Dragons are incredible intelligent beasts: wise, strong, ancient, and commanding. Their power is legendary; so many tales exist of a dragon acting as primal adversary, ancient guardian, or source of sovereign authority. If the dragon favors you, vast riches can be yours, and woe to those who would try to harm you.

To Call a Dragon

Remember that dragon energy is untamed and cannot be forced, owned, or commanded; it can only be invited in appropriately. To begin, make sure you have silenced your phone and will be undisturbed for a short period. If you have a figure or image of a dragon, keep it on hand to help in the visualization. Surround yourself in an energetic circle in order to create the proper magical environment. When you are ready, close your eyes and mentally visualize a land of dragons. See a mystical realm existing as a plane higher and lighter than our own in the upper atmosphere encircling the planet.

When this visualization is strong, call out to a dragon companion and see one making itself known. Envision this dragon coming toward you and speak to it. Tell it honestly what you desire. Ask for an alliance and a positive relationship with the dragon realm and this particular dragon especially. Inquire what the dragon would like from you in exchange for their assistance and commit to memory what they say. Alliances are two-way streets; we must give as much to the relationship as we seek from it. Thank the dragon for this contact and ask how they wish to be contacted in the future. Bid them farewell and visualize yourself returning to your own realm and open your eyes.

After this working, you may or may not feel the dragon's presence in your immediate environment. With continued contact, their presence will become more apparent and the connection strengthened. They can become powerful guardians and allies.

Simmering Potpourris

This pungent potpourri cleanses the atmosphere and balances the energy in the home so that more loving vibrations are felt.

SPICY SUMMER POTPOURRI

1 tablespoon black pepper (protection)

4 tablespoons basil (love, banishing, wealth)

3 tablespoons sugar (love, purification)

1 teaspoon garlic, minced (purification)

1 tablespoon lemon juice (purification)

1 tablespoon butter (faery work, transformation)

Water

Fill a pot half full with water and add the remaining ingredients. Simmer over low heat to release the scent. If you wish, this potpourri can actually be a good marinade/brine for soaking chicken before grilling for a summer meal. In this case, place the desired amount of chicken in a bowl or baking dish (with high sides) and soak the chicken in the marinade; cover in the refrigerator for 6 hours to overnight. Remove from marinade and grill according to preferred method, usually on a hot grill, skin side down for

3 to 5 minutes, then 50 to 60 minutes on a medium-heat grill, turning halfway through cooking time.

Brews

Much of kitchen witchery is about understanding how powerful what we already do is; the simple act of sipping sun tea can be a truly magical act when done with the proper intention. Tea is naturally attuned to prosperity as are the other ingredients in this recipe.

TASTE OF SUMMER PROSPERITY POTION

3 tea bags (prosperity)

1 peppermint tea bag (money, healing)

1 orange (prosperity)

2 quarts water

Honey, to taste (prosperity)

Slice the orange and place in a gallon jug. Add the tea bags and water. Charge the mixture with your intention. Place in direct sunlight for at least two hours. Strain tea and add the honey. Refrigerate for a few hours until cold. Serve over ice.

Incense

To fully enjoy the summer season, we must be clear of unneeded blockages or problems. This incense is attuned to the power of summer and also helps purify and restore a pleasant balance.

SUMMER SIZZLE INCENSE

1 teaspoon sage (protection, prosperity)

1 peppermint tea bag (purification, healing)

1 teaspoon basil (love, banishing)

1 teaspoon rosemary (love, purification)

1 teaspoon thyme (healing, purification)

1 teaspoon tarragon (protection, purification)

Open the tea bag and pour out the contents into a bowl. Add the remaining ingredients and stir to combine. Charge the incense to clear away incorrect energy and replace it with love, health, and prosperity.

Oils

Summer is not only the season of the largest amount of heat and light, but also magically speaking the time of the greatest development for abundance and prosperity. Whether we are actively connected to the agriculture cycle or not, all of humanity is inextricably linked to the growth of food, and most of what we eat comes into fullness at this time. The oil formula for the summer solstice given here taps into not only the solar energy of the holiday, but the energy of prosperity and luck as well to help manifest abundance in all forms.

SUNSHINE OIL

1 tablespoon sunflower seeds (luck)

1 tablespoon cashews (prosperity)

1 tablespoon peanuts (prosperity)

½ cup sesame oil (money, opportunity)

If a peanut allergy is a factor, they can be substituted with a teaspoon of cinnamon. If the smell of sesame oil is too unpleasant (to me it smells burnt), this too can be substituted; safflower or corn oils can be used instead. To prepare, crush the seeds and nuts together and add them to a pot with the oil. Warm over low heat until you begin to smell it in the air and remove from heat. Allow the oil to cool, strain it, and charge it by visualizing the bright noonday sun sending a beam of light down into the oil, infusing it with power.

SEA SPRITE OIL

This formula can be used to call upon the power of the mermaid and in any magic related to the sea.

½ cup grapeseed oil (moon magic)

Pinch sea salt (blessings)

2 tablespoons seaweed (crumbled sushi wrappers)
   (sea magic)

The seaweed wrappers should be easy to find. Whether dulse, nori, kelp, or another form, use what is available. Warm the oil and other ingredients over low heat until you smell the seaweed in the air (an unmistakable scent) and then remove from heat. Once cooled, strain into a bottle and charge it with the intent of sea magic and mermaid power.

Fire Dragon Oil

Attracting the energy and power of dragons is the focus of this oil recipe.

3 asparagus spears (dragon magic)

1 teaspoon basil (abundance, dragon magic)

1 teaspoon tarragon (dragon magic, protection)

½ cup sunflower oil (fire magic, strength)

The humble asparagus is distantly related to dragon's blood, the legendary ingredient related to love, protection, and power. Basil has an excellent attraction power, even to dragon energies, and tarragon is related to their magic as well. The sunflower oil can be substituted with corn oil if need be. Warm the oil and other ingredients over low heat until you can smell the herbs in the air. Remove from heat and charge to be a carrier of dragon magic and attraction then strain and bottle for use.

Charms

Far from being merely a place to buy food, our modern supermarkets (especially those "supercenter" places) have so many extra items like books, toys, kitchen appliances, and sometimes clothing and sunglasses. This last item can be charmed magically to increase protection and clear vision so that danger can be more easily spotted and avoided.

MAGICAL SUNGLASSES

1 pair sunglasses

1 red candle (fire)

Bowl of water (water)

Summer Sizzle incense (air)

Bowl of salt (earth)

Incense charcoal

Incense burner

On an altar table, set the bowl of salt in the north, the incense burner in the east, the candle to the south, and the bowl of water to the west. Hold the sunglasses in your hands and focus on the idea that they will bring protection and clarity to their wearer. Hold the glasses briefly over the incense, the candle, the water, and the salt to absorb the elemental energies and say:

Magical vision, forever ensured,
to wearer of these glasses, protection imbued;
keen, clear sight, shall be absorbed,
and each time worn, the power renewed.

Leave the sunglasses in the middle of the table to continue to absorb the elemental energy until the candle burns out. Wear as desired.

Foods

As children, it is unlikely that any of us ever imagined that roasted marshmallows had any magical potential, but they do. The sugar, gelatin, and egg whites found in many marshmallow recipes relate magically to love, purification, and binding, and the act of roasting adds the element of rejuvenation. Roasting marshmallows blesses them with fire's power and combining them with chocolate and graham crackers can turn humble s'mores into a magical goldmine of love, prosperity, or abundance.

MAGICAL WISHING MARSHMALLOWS

1 bag marshmallows (love, rejuvenation)

Chocolate bars (love, prosperity)

1 box graham crackers (abundance)

Roast the marshmallows over the stove or a fire and focus upon your magical goal. When the marshmallow is ready combine it with the chocolate in between two graham crackers and eat them to bring the magic within.

Bath Salts
This mixture is overflowing with the energy of summer, plus the power of love, purification, and luck.

Citrus Summer Bath Salt
1½ cups sea salt

¾ cup Epsom salt

¼ cup baking soda

½ teaspoon orange extract (love, luck)

½ teaspoon lemon extract (purification, love)

½ teaspoon vanilla extract (love, energy)

Mason jar

Mix the Epsom salt, sea salt, and baking soda in a bowl to combine. Add the extracts, stir, and pour into a jar. Holding your hands over it, charge the bath salts with purification and blessing energies. Put the lid on the jar. Use as desired.

Holiday: Midsummer
Aside from celebrating the power of the season and the divine powers beyond, this time of year is excellent for magic. The summer solstice holiday is one of peak magical

power. Most spells cast now have an extra boost of power, a special added "oomph" that helps them manifest in more satisfying ways. Whether you choose to add specific spells into the Midsummer celebration or decide to simply honor the energetic shift and enjoy the holiday, the longest day of the year can bless you with warmth and abundance.

Ritual

The rites of Midsummer are frequently focused on honoring the goddess of the earth. Thanks are given for her granting abundance; she is celebrated as queen of faery and sovereign of the land. The archetypal earth goddess (speaking in nondenominational terms) is seen as the creative power of nature's bounty, and the archetypal earth (and/or sun) god is seen as both the catalyst and embodiment of the created bounty. He is considered at the peak of his power, which is tied to both that of the sun and the crops. As the season continues and moves toward harvest, he is seen as waning in power and preparing to travel through the gates of death. The goddess is seen as eternal, changing her form but always maintaining her authority, and the god is seen as bound directly to the cycles of life in our world.[14]

This holiday celebrates life, abundance, strength, light, joy, and the fullness of nature's gifts coming to fruition. Given the warm temperatures and sunny days, midsummer

14   Janet and Stewart Farrar, *The Witches' Bible Compleat* (New York: Magickal Childe, 1984), 94–95.

is one of the ideal sabbats to hold outdoors. If close neighbors are a concern, what to all outward appearances is a simple backyard dinner around a firepit, can actually be a powerful sabbat ritual that doesn't draw too much attention or suspicion. Indoors, this ritual can be fully embellished and just as powerful as if it were outdoors.

THE DRAGON AND THE MERMAID OF MIDSUMMER

This rite connects to not only the qualities of abundance, the faery kingdom, and the sun, but also to the primary elements at play during this season: fire and water.

Sea Sprite oil

Fire Dragon oil

1 red candle

1 white candle, optional

Cauldron or black bowl

1 tablespoon sea salt in small cup

Water

Plate of blueberries (earth)

Plate of mushrooms (air)

Pineapple (fire)

Plate of peaches (water)

On a low table, place the unlit red candle that has been anointed with Fire Dragon oil as well as the lit white candle (which is being used solely for illumination). This table becomes the fire dragon altar. To the west of this altar, set the cauldron on the ground (or another low table) and fill it with water and a float a few drops of Sea Sprite oil on the surface; this becomes the mermaid water altar/focal point. Facing north, you now have a water altar on the left and a fire altar on the right in a similar manner to the twin bonfires sometimes seen at Beltane or the summer solstice. Moving to the quarters; set the plate of blueberries at the north point. To the east, place the dish of mushrooms; the pineapple goes at the southern point, and the peaches sit in the west. These are part of the bounty of summer and each are aligned to the element in their particular quadrant: earth, air, fire, and water, respectively.

Anoint your right wrist with Fire Dragon oil and your left wrist with Sea Sprite oil. As you begin the ritual, close your eyes and envision a large orb of light encircling your working area to just beyond where the fruits are placed. After this energetic circle is placed, light the red candle and say:

> *Here I light the dragon candle*
> *to invoke its ancient power.*
> *Fiery guardian of the land,*
> *help me to create the vision I see.*

Balance the heat and light for growth,
letting abundance now come forth.

Turn your attention to the cauldron and sprinkle a little bit of the sea salt into the water as you call to the spirit of the mermaid, saying:

Protector of the seas, guardian of the waters;
I call the mermaid from the depths.
Great water spirit, hear my plea,
quench the thirst of the land
and keep the balance toward prosperity.

Addressing both the guardians with gratitude say:

Sacred fire and water,
held in trust by dragon and mermaid,
balance the power that all may prosper
and protect us that we may live unafraid.

To conclude the ritual, thank the guardians for their blessings in your own words and say, "The strength of the sun is at its peak and the earth is warmed by this power, the land shall be rich with wonderful bounty. My thanks to the otherworld for these gifts, blessed be." The candle can be extinguished and the water can be poured upon the land. The fruits can be eaten as part of the sabbat feast.

If you are celebrating outdoors, a fire pit can stand in for the candle and a large bucket of water (which to all outward appearances could be for dousing the fire) can substitute for a cauldron. The fruit can still be placed in the directions even if only around the fire, and the magical oil can be added to the fire before it is lit. The words can be thought instead of spoken and the sabbat still enjoyed.

Witchy Ways

Because this time of year gets so hot and travel increases so much, it can be difficult to keep food cold on long trips. Ice packs can be helpful but are annoying to lug around after they have fully thawed. A great dual-purpose item to keep things cool is to freeze those little juice boxes and stick a few of them into your cooler along with the rest of the food. That way, your picnic lunch or travel snacks will stay cool. And when the juice boxes have thawed, instead of having extra plastic to haul around, you have something to drink.

Midsummer Shopping List

- Asparagus
- Baking soda
- Basil
- Blueberries
- Butter
- Candles, blue, white, and red
- Cashews
- Chocolate

- Epsom salt
- Garlic
- Graham crackers
- Grape seed oil
- Hazelnut oil
- Honey
- Lemon extract
- Lemon juice
- Marshmallows
- Mason jar
- Mushrooms
- Orange extract
- Oranges
- Peaches
- Peanuts
- Pepper, black
- Peppermint tea
- Pineapples
- Rosemary
- Sage
- Sea salt

- Sea weed
- Sesame oil
- Sugar
- Sunflower oil
- Sunflower seeds
- Sunglasses
- Tarragon
- Tea, black
- Thyme
- Vanilla extract

CHAPTER 11

The First Harvest

Though the summer solstice represents the peak of solar power and the hours of daylight begin to wane with each day that passes until Yuletide, the remainder of the summer season is still quite filled with heat and light. Generally speaking, the month of August is frequently the hottest month of the year and the daylight hours linger until around nine o'clock in the evening. This environment gives a perfect setting for outdoor get-togethers and reaping the rewards of summer's bounty. As the season moves forward, we are given the opportunity to begin to gather the fruits of our labors and once again pause in celebration, this time for the sabbat of Lughnasadh.

Stepping into Potential

If you cast the Essentials of Life spell back in May, you can now strengthen it with further magic to draw back your intention as it condenses into manifestation. Even if the previous spell has already resulted in reaching your goal, this spell can still be performed to seal the intention, thus ensuring that your magic will be maintained. As noted in the prior spell, fire, water, salt, and milk are viewed in this magic as life essentials. They were honored in the first working and in doing so, an intention was released. Now, they will be brought together in sacrifice to represent the effort needed to claim our goal.

Releasing the Essentials of Life

1 red candle (fire, abundance)

1 tablespoon salt, from the same
salt used before (blessing)

1 cup milk (nourishment)

Fill a bathtub with water at your preferred temperature. The water represents sustenance. Light the candle and place it near the bathtub where it will be safe but also within your reach from the tub. Step into the bath and pour in the milk and salt. Soak and feel the energies of the water, milk, salt, and flame absorbing into your body. Bask in these energies and speak your desire. When you are ready, pull the plug and as the water begins to drain, say this spell:

Fire, water, milk, and salt of earth,
I've kept your power close to me;
now to let my goal come forth,
I release the essentials and set them free.

Sprinkle some of the remaining water onto the flame of the candle to extinguish it. Once the water has completely drained, stand and rinse off the excess residue from the milk and salt.

HOLIDAY: Lughnasadh

The first thing that is usually discussed about this sabbat is that it is "the first harvest," but what does that mean? In her amazing book, *The Great Work*, author Tiffany Lazic describes the first harvest:

> *[It is] a reflection of the pre-spring purification, preparing for a time of activity and laying plans for the future. There is the gathering of harvest, but also the gathering of seeds that will be necessary for future harvests.* [15]

On the wheel of the year, Lughnasadh is the opposite day to Imbolc, and where on that holiday we prepare for the coming spring, at Lughnasadh we prepare for the coming autumn.

At this time, the very first gleanings of the harvest are gathered such as the first round of squash, early tomatoes,

---

15   Tiffany Lazic, *The Great Work* (Woodbury, MN: Llewellyn Publications, 2015), 239.

green beans, and so forth. Figuratively, this time is for gathering the resources from our accomplishments, making sure we will have enough available to ensure survival through the long winter. For modern practitioners, this would be a good time to take an accounting of financial matters to see if any changes need to be made. This holiday is one of feasting, games, and joy akin to the Mardis Gras festivities which are the revelries prior to the Christian period of Lent, the period of repentance, penance, and self-denial. I'm not saying that we need concern ourselves with any form of self-denial; I only want to point out that Lughnasadh is a celebration that occurs right before a time of great effort.

We work to secure what we need and maintain our lives and lands. Making sure that the rent money is in the bank is as much securing our sovereign land as the building of a stone boundary marker was three hundred years ago; the action takes many forms but has essentially the same goal. Since the main themes of Lughnasadh are abundance, sovereignty, preparation, and happiness, the recipes that follow are attuned to these energies.

Simmering Potpourris

This is admittedly a weird one but it actually works. If you would like to infuse your home with the quintessential energy of late summer, this is a fast and effective method. The best part? You can eat the results!

August Corn Potpourri

4 ears corn (luck, protection)

2 teaspoons sea salt (blessing, protection)

Water

Remove the husks and silk from the corn and rinse it clean. In a large pot, bring water to boil. Add the salt and then add the corn, cooking until tender, 5 to 10 minutes. Remove the corn from the water with tongs and set aside. Add the husks and silk to the pot and turn the heat down so that it just simmers. You can leave the pot simmering for as long as desired, adding water if needed.

Serve the cooked corn with butter, as it can become food magic for luck, protection, and transformation.

Brews

The sun's warmth and radiance is captured within this light and refreshing summer brew. This recipe can be doubled or tripled if you enjoy it and wish to use if for the ritual beverage for the holiday.

Lughnasadh Light Potion

1 tea bag, black (prosperity, courage)

1 chamomile tea bag (love, prosperity)

2 tablespoons pineapple chunks (luck, prosperity)

1 teaspoon basil (love, prosperity)

1 orange, sliced (love, prosperity)

3 cups water

Heat the water until bubbles form on the bottom of the pot, then remove from heat. Add the remaining ingredients and steep for 10 minutes. Strain and charge as a drink for Lughnasadh. Serve over ice, sweetened with honey if desired.

Incense

The magic of this incense not only includes connecting to the energy of the Lughnasadh sun but also the energies of love, abundance, healing, protection, and even warding against harmful forces. In keeping with this holiday, we are combining a wide variety of ingredients together to make something powerful without taking too much from any one thing; the small amounts creating (more than) enough for all.

Least of Enough Incense

1 tablespoon basil (love, money, banishing)

1 tablespoon rosemary (all-purpose)

1 teaspoon apple peel, dried (love, healing)

¼ teaspoon barley (love, protection)

Pinch whole wheat flour (abundance, fertility)

Combine the ingredients and grind the herbs together. Charge with your intention and bottle for use.

Oils

Since we have not yet had autumn's full harvest, we must make do with what we have. As we are just beginning to gather our abundance, we must be careful of what we use and be thrifty, using only what we need.

LEAST OF ENOUGH OIL

1 teaspoon brown rice (money, protection)

1 teaspoon quinoa (healing, fertility)

1 teaspoon chicory (prosperity)

1 teaspoon cashews (luck)

1 hazelnut (wisdom)

2 bay leaves

½ cup corn oil

Chicory may be difficult to find. It is a main ingredient in coffee substitutes. In the coffee aisle, there are usually one or two brands of coffee substitutes available. If you cannot find any, a teaspoon of chopped dates is a reasonable substitute. Combine all the ingredients and warm them in a pot. Once warmed, strain the oil, charge it, and bottle for use.

Powders

Grains in some form are a staple food of nearly every society: rice, wheat, corn, millet, and even quinoa have been used to nourish the world for thousands of years. This powder combines several grains that are linked to this time of year to draw in the energy of Lughnasadh and is also perfect for magic focused on protecting and maintaining abundance.

Flour Power Powder

1 tablespoon whole wheat flour (abundance)

1 tablespoon rice flour (abundance)

1 tablespoon oat flour (abundance)

1 tablespoon barley flour (protection)

Combine the flours and charge them with your intent. Use to encircle candles, create symbols, or draw the Lughnasadh circle (though the recipe will have to be multiplied).

Charms

The charm bag shown here is a quick way to infuse a large amount of ingredients with a one-time action. Popcorn naturally corresponds to improving luck and protection, and this can be focused and enhanced through our power and intention.

Popcorn Good Luck Charm

Cheesecloth

Kitchen twine or thread

Jar of unpopped popcorn (luck, protection)

Kitchen shears

Holding the jar of popcorn, charge it with the energy of luck and protection. Doing so will empower the entire jar with this intent. To create a separate, portable charm, layer two squares of cheesecloth on top of each other and set 3 tablespoons of the popcorn in the center. Pull up the corners of the cloth and using the twine, tie into a bundle, triple knot the twine and snip the ends of both the string and the cheesecloth to create a little bundle that will be a charm of luck and protection you can carry with you.

The jar can be stored as usual. To use, you can simply make popcorn in the usual manner and enjoy the benefits of magical popcorn; a healthy, luck-bringing, and protective snack.

Foods

Most of the foods of Lughnasadh are of the picnic or outdoor barbecue variety: salads, meats, breads, and fresh fruits. One of the crops that is ready to harvest at this time of year is a melon that is perfectly attuned to the sun and the magic of the season: the cantaloupe.

LITTLE BALLS OF SUNSHINE

2 whole cantaloupes (healing, protection)

1 peppermint tea bag (healing, abundance)

2 tablespoons sugar (purification)

Pinch of sea salt (blessing)

Melon baller

Large spoon

Large bowl

Cut the cantaloupes in half and scoop out the seeds and pulp. Using the melon baller, scoop out little balls from the melons and place them in the bowl. Sprinkle with the sugar and add the pinch of salt, stirring with the spoon. Open the tea bag and crumble the peppermint leaves over the melon balls and stir again to combine. Charge with intent and serve.

P.S. If you would like to infuse alcohol into the melon balls, you can combine ½ cup of vodka with ½ cup of pear juice and pour the mixture over the melons, stirring to coat. Refrigerate the melon, covered, for at least two hours before serving to allow everything to marinate together.

Bath Salts

A little luck, protection, and dissolution of any harmful energies that may be around you are the attributes of this bath salt. It is attuned to the power of the sun and is ideal for the Lughnasadh pre-ritual bath.

SUNFIRE BATH SALTS

1½ cups sea salt

¾ cup Epsom salt

¼ cup baking soda

1 teaspoon corn oil (luck, protection)

1 teaspoon sunflower oil (luck)

1 teaspoon safflower oil (hex breaking)

Mason jar

Combine the dry ingredients in the bowl and the oils in a smaller bowl. Pour the oils into the salt mixture and stir to blend. Charge with intent and bottle for use.

Witch Bottles

Much of the work and lore surrounding this "first harvest" is more about preparation than actual gathering. One way we can prepare for the main harvest at the autumn equinox, magically speaking, is to create clear intention of what you would like to harvest at that time. A simple way to do this is to write your wishes on paper and place them into a bottle. Keep the bottle, adding wishes to it as the season progresses if you like, creating a potent receptacle of focused energy for your desires.

HARVEST WISHES BOTTLE

Bottle with lid

8 teaspoons sage (wish magic)

8 hazelnuts (wish magic)

Paper and pen

Charge the sage to be a catalyst for your wishes to manifest and pour it into the bottle. Charge the hazelnuts for the same purpose and place them in the bottle over the sage. Write a wish on paper and roll it up like a scroll. Place the scroll into the bottle. Write as many wish scrolls as you want, being sure to only write one wish per paper, and when you are finished put the lid on the bottle and set it where you will see it often but it will not be handled by others.

Ritual

The primary themes honored and expressed in this Lughnasadh ritual shall be acknowledging the beginning of harvest, creating an offering to ensure a bountiful second harvest, feasting on the fruits of our labors, and cooling the heat of the sun. The sun, though a vitalizing force throughout spring and early summer, by this time has turned into a potentially destructive force for the all-important crops.[16] It is for this reason that a sympathetic act of magic can be

---

16   Lora O'Brien, *Irish Witchcraft from an Irish Witch* (Franklin Lakes, NJ: New Page Books, 2005), 167.

done in order to ensure that the heat of the sun will not destroy what we have worked so hard to create and nurture (literally or figuratively). It is also a traditional practice to compete in games of skill at this time and that too could be incorporated into your holiday celebration if you wish.

RELEASING THE HEAT OF HARVEST

Least of Enough oil

Least of Enough incense

Whole grain bread

Cup of water

Cauldron (for indoors)

Incense charcoal (for indoors)

1 white candle (for indoors)

Fire pit with fire (outdoors)

If you are working indoors, the cauldron with the incense charcoal smoldering inside and a white candle nearby shall constitute the Lughnasadh fire. If outdoors, a fire pit with a small fire can be kindled with the incense added to it as an offering. Prior to the ritual, anoint each wrist, the back of the neck and your "third eye" area with the Least of Enough oil. Have a plate of bread on the altar of if outdoors, on a nearby table along with the bottle of incense. Light the charcoal (or fire) and candle just prior to beginning the rite.

To begin, pour some of the incense from the bottle into your hand. Mentally envision the cycle of the life of plants from seed, to sprout, to sturdy plant and now the beginning of ripening; the downturn just before harvest. When you are ready, sprinkle the incense onto the coal or flame and say, "Here begins the first harvest, it is time to reap the rewards. Though much work is still before us, success as our fate lies in store." Pick up a piece of the bread. If necessary, you can use a barbecue fork for this task. Acknowledge to yourself how important the agricultural cycle is to the world even if you do not personally grow crops. See the bread as the first gleanings of harvest and freely offer the first portion back to the otherworld in thanks and hope for further bounty. If indoors, blacken a bit of the bread in the flame of the candle and set it in the cauldron. If outdoors, blacken the bread by dropping it into the fire. Either way, as it blackens say, "Through sprout and growth and maturity, the fruits of the harvest come to bear; in thanks and hope for continued abundance, this offering to the Gods, I freely share."

In your own words, give thanks for what you have been given in your own life and ask for help in whatever projects or spells you feel important, offering more incense if desired. After this, bless the rest of the bread. Holding your hands over it say, "May this bread nourish the body, mind, and spirit." Take a piece of the bread and eat it as a symbolic taking in of the power of the day and feasting upon the fruits of the first harvest. Eat as much or as little of the bread as you wish before concluding the ritual.

When you decide to end the rite, stand before the fire or cauldron holding the cup of water. In your own words, thank any deities with whom you work for the harvest and their support. Hold the cup high in salute and say, "Power of the sun, life-giving force, I ask that you do not destroy; I quench the heat of your fiery course, to preserve the harvest we must enjoy. This water is poured to cool the flame and shift the wheel to autumn's reign." Pour the water into the fire or cauldron. Extinguish the candle by sprinkling some of the water onto the flame. Now is the time for the Lughnasadh feast.

Witchy Ways

Whether or not you buy in bulk, it is a helpful idea to decant your dry goods into large jars. In this way, you can not only easily see what you have on hand, but the ingredients stay fresher sealed in a jar than they would in the usual paper or plastic sacks that most dry ingredients are sold in at the store. It is a good idea to label each jar with the name of the ingredient it holds to avoid accidentally mixing them up. If you want, even the labeling can be a magical act. Along with the name, you can draw an appropriate symbol for they type of energy contained in the food and empower the label with intent. As you place the label on the jar, fix within your mind that it will act as a magical charger; a catalyst to keeping that ingredient charged with the appropriately programmed energy, and you will have your pre-charged ingredients to add a touch of magic to all your cooking and baking.

Lughnasadh Shopping List
- Apples
- Baking soda
- Barley
- Basil
- Bay leaves
- Bread, whole grain
- Candles, red
- Cantaloupes
- Cashews
- Chamomile tea
- Cheesecloth
- Chicory
- Corn
- Corn oil
- Epsom salt
- Flour, wheat
- Hazelnuts

- Kitchen shears
- Kitchen twine
- Mason jars
- Milk
- Oat flour
- Oranges
- Peppermint tea
- Pineapple
- Popcorn
- Quinoa
- Rice, brown
- Rice flour
- Rosemary
- Safflower oil
- Sage
- Sea salt
- Sugar
- Sunflower oil
- Tea, black

SECTION 4

AUTUMN HARVEST

Now is the time of the main harvest season, with dry, cooler nights and the shifting of color into the bright shades of the newly falling leaves. The wild berries are now fully ripe and are another burst of color amid the backdrop of the remaining greenery. After the intense heat of late summer, the longer nights and milder temperatures of autumn can be welcome relief. For others, this seasonal shift can be a foreboding time; hinting at the approaching cold of winter. In either case, this is an essential season in the agricultural sense, for without the harvest we could not make it through the barren wintertime.

CHAPTER 12

Power of Autumn

It is clear that autumn's most significant theme is that of harvest, but another important facet of this time is that of balance. Much like the spring equinox, the autumnal equinox is a time of (nearly) equal day and equal night and the return to balance makes possible the richness of opportunity which is the harvest; both themes are intertwined. Though this time is one of the balance of light and dark, heat and coolness, it quickly shifts into the decline of the sun's energy and influence.

We can take this time to not only gather what we need to ensure a comfortable winter, but also to take stock of our current supplies. We can make sure that what we already have is readied, secured and properly accounted for so that we know what we have and what we need. Practically speaking, in our modern lives, this usually amounts to a thorough cleaning spree.

Spring Cleaning Again?

Not exactly spring cleaning but cleaning and storing our gardening tools, outdoor supplies, and recreational accessories readies our homes and lives for the abundance of harvest and a more efficient time navigating through winter. This is an excellent time to carefully clean garden shears, hedge clippers, lawn mowers, bicycles, sports equipment, and recreational vehicles; anything that will not likely be used though fall and winter. Having things cleaned before they are stored wards off rust and other damage and also ensures a smoother transition back to spring when you need these item again.

Reap Rewards

This is the final part of the long-term success magic that was begun near Beltane. It is the culmination; claiming our manifestation.

Bringing Together the Essentials of Life

1 orange candle (solar power, abundance)

Bottle of salt, the same salt from the earlier spell (blessing)

½ cup milk (nourishment)

¼ cup water (sustenance)

2 cups flour (abundance)

1 tablespoon baking powder (blessing)

8 tablespoons butter (transformation)

Light the orange candle to represent the fire element, place it nearby. Preheat the oven to 450° F. In a large bowl, stir together flour, baking powder, and ½ teaspoon of the salt from the bottle. Cut in the butter with two forks or a pastry blender (or throw all this into a food processor and pulse) until the mixture resembles coarse crumbs. Stir in the milk and water to make a soft dough. Turn dough onto a floured board and lightly knead until dough is no longer sticky. Roll out to a thickness of ½ inch and cut out biscuits with a biscuit cutter or a floured glass. With a sharp knife, cut a pentagram on top of each biscuit, charging them with prosperity. Place on a baking pan and bake for 10 to 20 minutes until golden brown. Cool on a wire rack. When the biscuits are ready, eat at least one while consciously taking into yourself the energy of abundance and acknowledging that you have created a physical manifestation of this process by turning the intention into this food. After you have eaten, bury at least one biscuit in the ground or a flowerpot as an offering of gratitude.

Holiday: The Witches' Thanksgiving

The autumn equinox holiday occurs during the midst of the harvest when we are gathering vegetables, fruits, and grains so that we may survive during the barren season of winter—or at least that's the standard tagline. For most of us, autumn means kids at school, cooler days, and getting home from work just before dark instead of at what feels like noon in the summertime. No matter which way of life we adhere to we are afforded the opportunity at the autumn equinox to pause for a moment and celebrate all that we have been given and reap the rewards of all our hard work throughout the year. This is the final holiday of the summer half of the year and the culmination of its power. The energy of balance and harvest are brought together at this point of power and the formulas given here help to channel these forces into our magic and our lives.

Simmering Potpourris

The warm spicy scent of this potpourri drifting through the air creates an atmosphere suitable for comfortable autumn evenings and harvest magic.

Autumn Warmth Potpourri

2 tablespoons pumpkin pie spice (love, abundance, protection, luck)

1 teaspoon cloves (love, protection)

2 cups apple cider (love, faery magic)

Warm the ingredients on the stove. Simmer for as long as desired, adding more apple cider or water if needed.

Brews

Though autumn helps to usher in the cooler time of the year, there is still much work to do and warm weather to experience, so a beverage that is ritually appropriate but still cold is a good choice. Two juices that are aligned with this holiday are cranberry and pomegranate, the latter being seen as an ancient fruit of the underworld.

Sparkling Autumn Brew

1½ cups pomegranate juice (luck, protection)

1 cup cranberry juice (protection, love)

1 cup club soda (energy enhancer)

Blend together the juices and charge with intent. Add the club soda and serve over ice.

Incense

The scent of this incense captures the feeling of autumn in such a way that only a campfire in the woods could match.

Autumn Equinox Incense

1 tablespoon sage (prosperity, protection)

2 teaspoons basil (prosperity, love)

1 teaspoon allspice (prosperity, healing)

1 teaspoon rosemary (prosperity, protection)

1 teaspoon apple peel (love, faery magic)

Grind the ingredients together and charge with intent.

Oils

This oil recipe builds upon the incense formula to create "wearable autumn," an oil that can infuse you with the season's energy.

Wearable Autumn Oil

1 tablespoon sage (prosperity, protection)

2 teaspoons basil (prosperity, love)

1 teaspoon allspice (prosperity, healing)

1 teaspoon rosemary (prosperity, protection)

1 teaspoon apple peel (love, faery magic)

3 drops pomegranate juice (protection)

½ cup olive oil (peace)

Combine the ingredients together in a pot and warm over low heat until you smell the herbs in the air. Remove from heat and allow it to cool before charging and bottling.

Powders

For the autumn season, grains of all kinds are a prominent ritual feature. This powder draws upon the power of the grains to form a protective powder that can be used in magic and ritual to protect from harm.

Harvest Powder

2 tablespoons cornmeal (protection)

2 tablespoons barley flour (protection)

2 tablespoons buckwheat (protection)

Blend the grains together and charge with protective energy. Bottle for use.

Charms

In some of the older harvest traditions, when the crops were being brought in, the last sheaf of grain to be reaped was kept and turned into a corn dolly. This was seen to embody the Cailleach (kal-yach) as the power of the harvest. Though we may not have ready access to a sheaf of grain from the local market, we can create a similar charm out of easily accessible ingredients. This charm can be used to preserve the prosperity of the family through the dark half of the year.

Cailleach Sheaf Charm

1 spoon

2 tablespoons whole wheat kernels
   or flour (abundance, fertility)

Cheesecloth

Kitchen twine

Bless each of the ingredients to be protective of prosperity. Lay two squares of cheesecloth over each other. Place the spoon with the bowl of the spoon in the center and the handle pointed to one of the corners of the cheesecloth. Carefully pour the whole wheat kernels into the bowl of the spoon. Gently fold the cheesecloth down over the spoon to capture the grains and bowl of the spoon. Use the twine to tie under this bundle where the bowl meets the handle. This forms the head of the Cailleach. You can leave this as is or embellish by tying a popsicle stick across to form arms and using such items as corn husks to dress her up.

Bless the completed dolly to be a protective charm for the fortunes of your family and keep her safe throughout the winter. When spring arrives, you can bury the Cailleach (removing the spoon) in the earth with thanks to release the power back into the world so you can build upon the prosperity.

Foods

This colorful side dish is a delicious addition to an autumn feast.

Succotash

¼ cup olive oil (healing, peace)

3 tablespoons butter (transformation)

1 onion, chopped (protection)

2 cloves garlic (protection)

2 medium red peppers, seeded
and chopped (protection)

2 zucchini, diced (protection)

2½ cups lima beans, frozen (protection)

3 cups corn, frozen (protection)

Salt, to taste (blessing, protection)

Pepper, to taste (protection)

1 teaspoon thyme (purification)

1 teaspoon sage (protection)

Pinch basil (love, wealth, banishing)

Sauté the onion and garlic in a pan with the olive oil until
the onion is translucent. Add the red pepper, zucchini, and
the butter, stirring to blend. Next, pour in the lima beans
and corn, stirring once more. Season with the herbs and
salt and pepper, cook for 10 to 15 minutes until the mixture thickens slightly and the colors are vibrant, then remove from heat. Charge with intent and serve.

Bath Salts
This bath salt draws in the energy of autumn and also the
magic of protection.

Fruits of Harvest Bath Salt

1½ cups sea salt

¾ cup Epsom salt

¼ cup baking soda

1 teaspoon cran-raspberry juice (protection)

1 teaspoon pomegranate juice (protection)

Mason jar

Combine the dry ingredients and then stir in the juices. Use the 100 percent juice blends or make your own. Charge with intent and bottle for use.

Witch Bottles

During the harvest time, it is paradoxically appropriate to release things, patterns, and behaviors which no longer meet our needs. While this does not amount to an actual banishing, we can instead send them away with our blessing to find new purpose.

Sacrifice Ash Bottle

Mason jar or wide-mouth bottle with lid

Pen and pieces of paper

White candle

On the pieces of paper, write what you would like to release and then burn each paper separately in the flame of the candle, dropping them in the bottle to burn to ash. As each one burns, visualize the item being out of your life. Once all of the papers have been burned and cooled, place the lid on the jar. Keep the jar and use the ashes to mark symbols for other releasing or banishing work.

Ritual

The autumn equinox ritual is a time to give thanks for blessings received. A time of abundance, this ritual should be filled with good things; delicious food, good company, warmth, and happiness. The foods normally associated with the American Thanksgiving holiday work perfectly at this time: turkey, stuffing, mashed potatoes, cranberry sauce, pumpkin pie, apple pie, rolls, etc. Prepare as many favorite foods as feels appropriate for this ritual, blessing them as you make them.

Receiving the Blessing of Autumn

3 candles, green, brown, orange (fire, light)

Cup of red wine or apple cider for each
    person (blessings)

Chosen foods (nourishment, abundance)

Athame

On a larger, preferably round table, place the three candles in the center with the green one on the left, the orange one in the center and the brown one on the right. Another option besides the orange candle is a dark cranberry color. These candles not only symbolize the waning light of the sun, but also the shifting focus of nature and the changing leaves. If you cannot find these colors, three white candles will do.

Arrange the plates of food around the table and place the wine toward the center. Bless the cup of wine by lowering the athame into the cup (holding the cup over the bottle if necessary to bless it all), sending energy into it. Say:

> *Vessel of creation, elixir of life,*
> *union of spirit and flesh combine;*
> *liquid charged through cup and knife,*
> *pierce the veil and bless the wine.*

If the liquid is instead apple cider, the same blessing can still be used, holding the cup over the bottle to bless it all. After the beverage is blessed, each person is poured a cupful. When all the items have been placed on the table, everyone can sit down for a feast.

When everyone has prepared their plates, hold up the cup of wine in a toast and say:

> *Through the year we've worked hard and can now reap*
> *the fruits of our labor. I ask that we can fully claim the*
> *blessings of nature and good favor. Blessings to us all.*
> *May we thrive even through the time of decline and*
> *emerge renewed in the spring. So mote it be.*

Now eat the meal in reverence for the blessing of this abundance, reserving a portion to be buried in offering after dinner. At the conclusion of the feast, extinguish the candles with the intent that as the light goes out, we are walking freely into the dark half of the year, keeping our strength and abundance intact.

Witchy Ways

Any form of gourd has naturally protective qualities. If you buy decorative gourds and charge them to be magical protection, you can place one or more of them in each room to make a festive, inconspicuous magical ward. If you choose the hard gourds that dry out over time, these gourd wards can last for several years. To charge them, simply hold each gourd in both hands and visualize it charging with protective energies to guard your home.

Autumn Shopping List

- Allspice
- Apple cider
- Apples
- Baking powder
- Baking soda
- Barley flour
- Basil
- Buckwheat
- Butter

- Candles, orange, green, brown, and white
- Cheesecloth
- Cloves
- Club soda
- Corn, frozen
- Cornmeal
- Cranberry juice
- Cran-raspberry juice
- Epsom salt
- Flour, whole wheat
- Garlic
- Kitchen twine
- Lima beans, frozen
- Mason jars
- Milk
- Olive oil
- Onions
- Pepper, black
- Peppers, red
- Pomegranate juice
- Pumpkin pie spice

- Rosemary
- Sage
- Sea salt
- Thyme
- Wine, red
- Zucchini

CHAPTER 13

Summer's End

In the area where I live, the heat of summer doesn't fully break until the third week of October. Not being a fan of triple-digit temperatures (or anything above 75° F actually), it is a welcome relief when the heat dissipates and autumn finally takes hold. The leaves have barely begun to change color by this time and the clouds begin to drift through the cooling breezes, whisking away the clinging heat of the sun. Large displays of pumpkins await me at the supermarket, each one a potential jack o' lantern. My usual pattern is to buy one as soon as they are available and then buy one or two each week up until the big day.

Calling on the Ancestors

One of the hallmarks of the Samhain season is that it is a time when the veil between the worlds is thin and we may have greater connection to the otherworld. During this window of time, we can enhance our ability to contact out ancestors. Generally, there is a significant difference between our ancestors and the Ancestors; the first being the departed members of our immediate family that were known to us and the latter being the larger members of our tribe, community, or special group. Those special, powerful predecessors that originated our particular way of life and have spiral upward into the otherworld to be revered for their skill; ascended masters, if you will, are honored during this time and often at every holiday. Aside from calling them the Ancestors, those beings are sometimes referred to as "the Ancient Ones" (though this can have other meanings) or the "Hidden Company." [17]

Calling upon our departed loved ones is a process that has a great many fans but also has some detractors. Some people feel that these ancestors are best left alone to move through their own destinies and may not appreciate being summoned by us for a chat. [18] In that case, it is still a very appropriate practice to honor them and reflect upon their meaning in our lives. If however, the desire to make contact is strong, there are some gentle methods to try that are

---

17   Gwyn, *Light from the Shadows*, 231.
18   Scott Cunningham, *Wicca: A Guide for the Solitary Practitioner* (St. Paul, MN: Llewellyn Publications, 1988), 143.

not about coercion but instead require an atmosphere of cooperation from both sides.

Beacon of Light

Cup of blessed saltwater

Notebook and pen

Mementos from the one to be contacted

In a quiet place, settle yourself in a comfortable area. Sprinkle some of the saltwater in a circle around you, visualizing that it is dissolving any harmful energy, leaving only appropriate vibrations. Focus on the mementos and let your mind drift to happy, strong memories of the departed person. Allow yourself to slip into a meditative state, let your eyes close and begin to focus on where your loved one is *right now.* Feel as though you are sending out a beacon of shining light from where you are out into their realm and that this light shall act as a bridge for them to make contact. Visualize them in real time. Try to get a sense of what they may look like in spirit; don't force an image, simply allow it to form. Reach out with your feelings and speak to them, asking them to make a positive, enjoyable, mutually beneficial contact.

Continue to visualize them and after a time, they may begin to speak to you. Again, do not force what you think "should" occur, simply be receptive and allow things to unfold. Have a nice meeting and when it is time to part, commit what they have said to memory and bid them farewell. See them move back into their realm and withdraw the light back down. Open your eyes and write down as much as you remember of the contact.

Word of caution: If anything begins to take an uncomfortable turn, hold up your dominant hand, mentally assert yourself, and cut off the beam of light to immediately break the connection. Open your eyes and take a tiny sip of the salted water to ground and seal your energies.

Holiday: Samhain

Glowing jack o' lanterns, shrieking ghosts, fluttering bats, and spooky disembodied howling embody the atmosphere of the day. Hordes of goblins, monsters, superheroes, and cartoon characters flood the streets, seeking one particular type of treasure: candy. In the dark of night, Witches enact mysterious rituals to honor the sacred shifts in energy of the year. The power of Samhain is second to none; it is the highest of the high holidays, the Witches' grand sabbat. Though each holiday is theoretically of equal importance, this day has always held a higher significance to many Witches.

This time of year is considered the end of summer or the light half of the year and the beginning of winter or the dark half. It is the doorway from one year to another, hence it being considered the Witches' New Year. This is an important day when we can use magic to keep anything harmful from the past out of our futures.[19] It is a key time for change in that because we are entering a new cycle, we can magically project how we wish our lives to be for that time. This has implications in everything from costume choice to food selection and evening plans; we can make this night exactly how we want it and our futures to be.

This is also an excellent night for divination to look into the new year and see what our futures hold. Beyond our own concerns, we can also honor the ancestors (both the regular and capital "A"), acknowledge the dead in general, give thanks to the deities, and light the sacred fires for protection and reverence. Though this is an exciting, magical, and sacred time, there can be difficulties. Uninvited spirits or faeries can make themselves known, playing their pranks and being disruptive. If this happens, a house cleansing may be in order.

House Cleansing

A good basic house cleansing can be done with little more than an athame and a black candle.

Get Out Already

1 black candle in sturdy holder (banishing)

Athame

---

19   Laurie Cabot, *Celebrate the Earth* (New York: Delta, 1994), 13.

Beginning near your front door and moving clockwise through the house, go through each room holding the candle and athame, visualizing white light streaming from the knife, filling your home with positive energy so strong it pushes out anything incompatible. Go from room to room, making a clockwise circuit but also walking in a clockwise circle within each room. Trace a pentagram over each window and door. Each time you trace a pentagram, say, "Causing strife, not in harmony; I command you now, get out already!" When you have completed the circuit, extinguish the candle and once it has completely cooled, dispose of it outside in the trash.

Simmering Potpourris

The aroma of this potpourri drifting through the air on Samhain enhances the atmosphere for ritual and recreation. Tarragon and rosemary are key ingredients. Rosemary provides a powerful almost woodsy scent, and tarragon is related to both mugwort and wormwood, making it appropriate for this time of year.

HALLOWED AURA POTPOURRI

2 tablespoons tarragon (protection, purification)

2 tablespoons rosemary (purification, protection)

2 tablespoons sage (cleansing)

1 teaspoon cloves (love, prosperity)

1 cup apple juice (faery magic)

1 cup water

Combine all ingredients and simmer in a pot for as long as desired, adding more water if needed.

Brews

For the Samhain Witches' brew, you'll need a giant cauldron over a bonfire, the fruit of a dragon, and the black of night. If these things are unavailable, a better option is the following recipe—cackling optional, of course. This potion helps to open psychic awareness and can aid in communication with the otherworld and divination.

SAMHAIN PSYCHIC POTION

2 peppermint tea bags (psychic awareness)

1 bay leaf (clairvoyance)

¼ teaspoon cinnamon (psychic awareness)

¼ teaspoon nutmeg (healing, psychic awareness)

1 tablespoon pomegranate syrup/
  molasses (protection)

2 cups water

Heat the water and the first four ingredients in a pot until it just begins to boil. Remove from heat and strain. Stir in the pomegranate syrup and charge with intent before serving. If pomegranate syrup is not available, substitute 1 tablespoon pomegranate juice and sugar to taste.

Incense

This incense is designed to clear away old energy and pave the way for renewal. It is good for connecting with the energy of Samhain and for ridding yourself of negatives.

SAMHAIN FREEDOM INCENSE

2 teaspoons basil (banishing)

1 teaspoon sage (cleansing)

1 teaspoon tarragon (purification)

1 teaspoon thyme (purification)

1 teaspoon rosemary (purification)

Grind each of the herbs together and charge with the intent of banishing and the energy of Samhain.

INCENSE SPELL

This spell helps to banish specific things from your life. It should be used with care and for the good of all.

BANISHING OF NEGATIVITY

1 black candle

Cauldron

Samhain Freedom incense and incense charcoal

Paper and red pen

Light the candle and light the incense in the cauldron. On a piece of paper write what you wish to banish in red ink. Crumple up the paper and focus on what you have written leaving your life. Make this intent strong and when you are ready light the paper in the flame of the candle, drop it into the cauldron of incense, and say, "Dark of night and banishing smoke, your power of freedom I invoke; to rid me of what blocks my way, releasing me into bright new day." Extinguish the candle and incense, and when the ashes are cooled flush them down the toilet.

Oils
This oil can assist in both connecting to the energy of Samhain and also in calling upon departed ancestors in ritual.

ANCESTOR OIL
1 teaspoon rosemary (protection)

1 teaspoon sage (cleansing)

1 teaspoon tarragon (purification)

¼ teaspoon honey (healing, binding)

¼ teaspoon pomegranate juice (protection)

Pinch sea salt (blessing)

Pinch tobacco (purification)

Pinch mint (purification)

½ cup olive oil (healing, peace)

Warm the olive oil and the first five ingredients in a pot until you can smell the herbs in the air. Remove from heat and allow to cool. Strain the oil into a bottle and add the remaining ingredients. Charge with intent and use as needed.

Powders

During this time of natural decline, it is customary to wok magic for cleansing and banishing of negativity. The reason for this is not that this time of year is evil (far from it), but rather that it is the ending of one cycle and the beginning of the next. It creates a solid foundation for the new year if we remove the leftover residue of the past and replace it with the energy of blessing. It also keeps us secured from any incorrect or harmful forces that may be in the vicinity.

Banishing Powder

1 teaspoon cinnamon (success)

1 teaspoon black pepper (banishing)

1 teaspoon rosemary (banishing)

1 teaspoon sage (cleansing)

1 teaspoon garlic powder (banishing)

2 chamomile tea bags (peace)

1 teaspoon salt (blessing, protection)

Combine these ingredients and charge them to banish incorrect, unwelcome energies and forces. Bottle for use. To use: sprinkle at the threshold or on windowsills to keep evil or incompatible people and energies from entering.

Charms

The magic of Samhain is that of endless possibility. Since we return to the beginning, we can begin anew in any way we wish. This time is a cross quarter day, the day between seasonal shifts, and so is a crossroads. An important symbol of crossroads deities and their power to create change is the key. Keys symbolize being able to find new opportunity, to open doors. This charm uses a key blank from the store or an old key you no longer have a use for to create new opportunity.

KEY OF CHANGE

2 black candles

1 key

Ancestor oil

Samhain Freedom incense and incense charcoal

Cauldron or incense burner

Once you have obtained the chosen key (either a key blank from the store or an old unused key), soak it in blessed saltwater overnight to cleanse it of any disharmonious energy, then clean it in pure water and dry with a towel. Have a clear idea of what doorway you would like to open, what goal you want to reach. Anoint your wrists, back of neck, and third eye area with the Ancestor oil. Light the candles and incense. Pick up the key and focus on your goal. Anoint the key with the oil and say, "Doors of opportunity, shall now be open to me; powers of the crossroads, make open the way, that my goal is reached without delay." Hold the key briefly over the smoke of the incense and the flame of the candles. Keep the key with you, ideally on your regular keychain.

Foods

There are traditional foods used to honor the spirits that roam about on this night. Apples are one, black beans and fava beans are two others. Turnips too are a traditional food of this time and turnips were the original jack o' lanterns. This recipe can be used in the Samhain meal and also as a food offering to the ancestors.

ANCESTOR FOOD

2 turnips

2 apples

3 tablespoon olive oil

2 teaspoons oregano

1 teaspoon garlic, minced

1 tablespoon pine nuts

Pre heat the oven to 425° F. Slice the turnips and apples into wedges and coat with the olive oil. Toss with the oregano, pine nuts, and garlic, and spread in a baking pan. Roast until cooked through, about 30 minutes. Serve.

Bath Salts

Absorb the magic for wisdom, healing, and love with this Samhain bath salt, perfect for aligning with the sabbat energy before the ritual.

SAMHAIN BATH SALT

1½ cups sea salt

¾ cup Epsom salt

¼ cup baking soda

1 teaspoon hazelnut oil (wisdom)

1 teaspoon almond extract (wisdom)

¼ teaspoon apple juice (love, healing, faery magic)

Mason jar

Combine the dry ingredients in a bowl and add the oil, extract, and juice, stirring to combine. Charge with intent and bottle for use.

Witch Bottles

This bottle is designed to assist in calling upon a specific departed ancestor. It acts as a beacon to their energy and gives them a channel for contact.

Beacon of Love Bottle

Large wide-mouthed bottle or mason jar

Mementos of a departed loved one

Photographs of the person

In the bottle, arrange an attractive grouping of items that remind you of the departed person and give the feeling of strong connection. Charge the bottle with white light to be a beacon directly to the person and seal the bottle. Keep on or near the Samhain altar.

Ritual

This Samhain ritual connects to the ancestors and spirits, the wise crone, the power of protection for the home and land, and the magic of divination.

Hallowed Ground Ritual

2 "jack be little" pumpkins, properly prepared (healing, protection)

1 black candle

1 white candle

1 cup Samhain Psychic potion

Plate of bread or cookies

3 apples

Cauldron

Athame

Samhain Freedom incense and incense charcoal

Ancestor oil

Method of divination: tarot cards, pendulum, etc.

Jack be little pumpkins are those tiny pumpkins that fit in the palm of your hand. Get two of those and cut a hole in the top large enough to fit a candle, scooping out the stem and any seeds or pulp. In one pumpkin fit the black candle and in the other the white, placing the black one on the left and the white one on the right toward the rear of the altar. Place the three apples in the middle between the candles. Set the cauldron in the center with the incense charcoal inside it. The cup of potion goes just to the left of the cauldron and the athame on the right. The plate of bread or cookies is placed in front of the cauldron, and the divination medium is to the left of the plate.

To begin, light the candles and incense and use the athame to cast a magic circle around yourself and the working area, calling any guardians you choose. Anoint yourself with the Ancestor oil on the wrists, back of the neck, and the third eye. Close your eyes and focus on this night, the power and mystery of Samhain. In legend, the

Cailleach arises this night to bring forth the power of winter. She roams across the land, striking the ground with her hammer causing it to frost. The Cailleach is an ancient Celtic crone goddess of winter and of the land. Meditate on the magic of this time, the doorway to the otherworld being open and the focus of the land being shifted to the dark half of the year. Mentally reach out to the crone of wisdom (either the Cailleach or your own chosen deity) and ask her to bless you with strength and the power to thrive in the winter. If desired, ask her to open the doorway to allow communication with any chosen loved ones at this time. Ask her to bless and protect your home that it may be fit for magic and a safe haven throughout the year as witchly, hallowed ground.

Bless the bread with the words:

Samhain cakes for the dead,
I bless you now that all may be fed.
Partake of the magic of this night
and nourish the living with magical sight.

Take a drink from the cup of potion. If you wish to communication with the departed, speak directly to a chosen person and ask them to make themselves known through the divination method you have chosen. Ask questions and use the divination to find answers. When you have asked all your questions, thank them for coming to visit you.

In thanks, crumble some of the cookies or bread around the incense charcoal in the cauldron. Conclude the rite by holding up the cup in salute and saying:

> *May the blessings of Samhain be upon us all.*
> *Let the living meet with their beloved dead,*
> *homeward to commune may they be led.*
> *Crone of wisdom, bless this land*
> *with the time of rest and repose at hand.*
> *Keep us safe the winter through*
> *and let our magic manifest true.*
> *For good of all and blessed be,*
> *as I will so mote it be.*

Take another sip of potion and pour the rest into the cauldron, extinguishing the incense charcoal. Open the circle and extinguish the candles. Bury the contents of the cauldron along with at least one apple.

Witchy Ways

If you would like to combine modern festivities with old traditions, you can carve magical jack o' lanterns. Pumpkins are magically attuned to the moon, prosperity, and healing, so the jack o' lantern can be a very effective protective charm. They can be carved to resemble your totem animals or with elemental symbols, placed around the circle at the cardinal directions as both markers and guardians. You can also sprinkle the banishing powder into the bottom of the pumpkin to lend it extra potency to keep evil from entering your home or ritual area.

Samhain Shopping List
- Almond extract
- Apples
- Apple juice
- Baking soda
- Basil
- Bay leaves
- Bread or cookies
- Candles, black and white
- Chamomile tea
- Cinnamon
- Cloves
- Epsom salt
- Garlic
- Garlic powder
- Hazelnut oil
- Honey
- Key blank
- Mason jars

- Nutmeg
- Olive oil
- Oregano
- Pepper, black
- Peppermint tea
- Pine nuts
- Pomegranate juice
- Pomegranate syrup
- Pumpkins, jack be little
- Rosemary
- Sage
- Sea salt
- Tarragon
- Thyme
- Turnips
- Tobacco

SECTION 5

SPECIAL OCCASIONS

CHAPTER 14

Lunar Magic, Rarities, and Leap Day Enchantment

Since the lunar cycle is a monthly occurrence, I have chosen to present all the lunar information in one place to avoid repetition. Though many magical people choose to celebrate the different moons according to their astrological placement or traditional seasonal attributes, the primary essence of lunar energy remains a constant and it is this power which these formulas draw upon. This chapter will also focus on the more rare occurrences such as eclipses and double or "blue" moons, plus that special day that only happens once every four years—Leap Day.

The Power of the Moon

As the earth's only natural satellite, the moon has influence over the tides of the ocean. Since we are beings mostly made of water, it is thought that the shifts of the moon have an effect upon us as well. Spiritually speaking, the moon is considered a great focuser of astral energy; it absorbs, condenses, and channels stellar, planetary, and celestial energies that are sent to earth via the lunar light.[20] Without the moon to gather and channel these mystical forces, it is believed that magical practice would be much more difficult; the moon is the great facilitator, transferring the influences of the greater cosmos down to our world, enacting the Hermetic axiom: "As above, so below."

The lunar cycle is a process with a similar nature to the (usual) four seasonal divisions of the year. The new moon is a point in time, followed by the waxing crescent phase. Next comes the first quarter point, followed by the waxing gibbous phase and then the full moon point. The full moon is the peak and then comes the waning gibbous phase and last quarter point. The last phase is the waning crescent followed by the dark moon point. The points could be considered similar to the solstices and equinoxes as these are times of concentrated energies (both astrologically and magically) with the phase that follows considered the "season" they have brought forth.

---

20   Raven Grimassi, *Wiccan Magick* (St. Paul, MN: Llewellyn Publications, 1998), 97–99.

Magic worked according to lunar phase or cycle (regardless or form or intention) is inherently moon magic in that the spell sent into the astral plane is carried there through the medium of lunar energy. When casting a spell, we release our intention outward into the astral in order for it to gather strength, creating a strong enough form in that sphere that it then condenses into the physical world. When the moon is in the phase corresponding to the nature of our working, it generates the natural current that carries our intentions to their conclusion. This is one reason why different types of magic are timed to the moon phases or specific points in the lunar cycle.

New Moon

There are two definitions of "new moon," one literal and the other more symbolic. The literal time of the new moon is when the moon is aligned with the sun and not visible to the naked eye. The symbolic time of the new moon is a couple of days afterward when the thin crescent sliver of moonlight is seen in the western horizon at sunset. This first sighting of the moon in its fresh waxing cycle is the new moon.

The point of the new crescent moon begins the phase of growth, increase and beginning projects. That which is begun at this time tends to grow stronger in accordance with the waxing light of the moon. Magic such as healing (mending and regrowth), new love, employment, friendship, and so on are favored during this time. It is also an appropriate time to work with deities of increase such as goddesses and gods of the hunt and of agriculture.

First Quarter Moon

This point in the lunar cycle is the waxing half-moon, the perfect half-circle in the evening sky. Astrologically, this is a time when the moon is considered square (at a 90° angle) to the sun. This isn't the most propitious time for using magic to acquire something, as the energy does not flow as freely. It is, however, a good time to work magic to overcome a block or obstacle when trying to achieve a goal. Turning a corner and finding a new path to success is, oddly, favored now. It is also an ideal time to work with warrior deities as they can help you break through obstacles and conflicts.

Gibbous Moon

The gibbous moon is the phase in which the moon is "more than half." When I see her face at his time, it reminds me of those beautiful "lady pin" brooches that have a cameo of a woman's face on it usually covered partially by her hair, a veil, or a hat. This is similar to the moon at this time which is still partly obscured in shadow. This is a good time for magic for increase. The moon is almost full but still increasing (waxing) in power so the magic worked now follows suit. Working with any deity now for a positive purpose is favored.

Full Moon

The peak of lunar power! This is the point of the greatest output of light and energy cascading down to earth. We have at our disposal added energy and also greater natural ability to release our intent into the astral plane. We not only have increased access to the energy of the moon but also planetary and stellar energies, the moon being the magical gateway to connect to these powers. Any type of magic can be worked now for added potency as can psychic work and spiritual endeavors. It is also the key time to work with goddesses of all types, particularly the most ancient creator deities.

Disseminating Moon (Waning Gibbous)

The waning gibbous is just beginning its decrease, and so is good for magic that involves release. Spells cast in this regard will follow the lunar current and take away whatever is not desired as the moon continues to wane. Warrior deities such as Athene or Thor can help with this work.

Third Quarter Moon

This is the waning half-moon, the negative counterpart to the first quarter point in the cycle. The energy of this time is somewhat static but it is a good time for working to go around an obstacle. It is also good for working with warrior gods, again to overcome adversaries and obstacles and for achieving justice, though this should be done with care. It is considered unwise to call upon deities for petty or unjust purposes, and the specifics of what constitutes justice are best left to their judgment and according to the "for the good of all" ethical guideline.

Waning Crescent Moon

The time of the waning crescent is prime time for banishings, dissolution magic of all kinds, un-bindings, severing ties, and removing specific obstacles. A word of warning: it is not usually a good idea to cast a spell to "remove all obstacles" from your life as it isn't always clear what may be an obstacle, and sometimes you would rather keep some things in place rather than having your life turned upside down all at once with numerous concurrent changes. Removing obstacles should ideally be a specific, case by case effort, done carefully and with the ethical implications well in mind.

This is also a fantastic time for healing magic aimed at removing illness, reducing swelling, dissolving unwanted growths, and similar. If the healing involves removing, dissolving, or purging something from the body, now is the best time to do it. This can be helped by working with deities of healing and transformation.

Dark Moon

The dark moon is the point directly prior to (and including) the literal new moon. This is the time when the moon is traveling so close to the sun (from our perspective) that it cannot be seen. The final benchmark before the lunar cycle renews itself, the dark moon is a good time for divination; looking deep within and beyond at the most receptive and introspective time in the cycle. It is also a time to work with deities of the night; goddesses and gods of the dark, the underworld and otherworld, though some prefer to avoid magical activities at this time.

Occasionally, two dark moons occur during a single month and when this happens, the second dark moon is sometimes referred to as a black moon. The black moon can be an excellent time for practicing deep meditations, introspection, silence, and acknowledging and releasing anger and pain.

How This Relates to Magical Practice

Sometimes, we get stuck in a magical rut where we might not see a new option or pathway to reaching a goal. In terms of the lunar cycle and magical timing, this can cause a type of magical paralysis wherein we may choose to avoid taking action because it is the "wrong" time in the moon's cycle. While it is true that certain types of magic are better suited to the different phases, this need not be a hindrance to acting when needed. If properly considered, any goal can be successfully worked toward during any lunar phase. The secret is in how the goal is approached. For example, during the time of the waning moon, it is not generally favorable to cast a spell to seek employment, but it can be an excellent time to use magic on yourself to remove any disharmonious patterns to gaining employment: subconscious fears, bad habits, unprofessional behaviors, and so forth.

Conversely, during the waxing moon period it is not considered favorable to use magic for banishing or un-hexing, but it is perfect timing to work blessing magic strong enough to rid the problem all together. It is all about finding the right approach, a fact plainly evident regarding healing spells. As already shown, the type of healing most appropriate during the waxing phase is that of mending and regrowth. The waning moon phase is more suited to healing of the removing type—ridding the body of illness, swelling, or inflammation. Healing can be achieved in either phase; it is simply a matter of strategy and planning.

The Solar Eclipse

Astronomically speaking, a solar eclipse occurs when the orbit of the moon causes it to directly cross the path of the sun, blocking the solar rays and causing a shadow to form on the earth. Astrologically speaking, when this happens it is a perfect alignment (conjunction) of the sun and moon in the same zodiac sign. In astrology, because a solar eclipse only occurs during a new moon, it is considered to be a concentration of power, like a triple-strength new moon. This formation can create chaotic and disruptive energy that may be difficult, but it can also be harnessed to create important change.

This energy is not delicate—it is not the gentle warmth of a hearth fire on a cold winter's night; it is instead a powerful laser beam or the searing heat from a carefully focused magnifying glass that concentrates the sun's light into the force of fire. This energy should only be magically harnessed for magic designed to create a strong impact; when you want change to seemingly come out of nowhere, this is the aspect to choose.

The Lunar Eclipse

There are two divergent points of view regarding the lunar eclipse. The first view is actually a more recent development. The time during eclipse is considered a period of concentrated magic in which the moon, normally full at this time, instead experiences every phase at once as the shadow of the earth passes over it. In this sense it can be harnessed as a potent time for spellwork of nearly any purpose. The other point of view takes a different tack that considers the astrological difficulty in this lunar aspect.

Whereas a solar eclipse concentrates magical energies, a lunar eclipse can have a stifling and blocking effect. The lunar eclipse occurs when the earth passes between the sun and what would ordinarily be the moon's full phase. The shadow covering the moon belongs to the earth as it blocks the sun's rays. This blocking is a disruption of the usual order of things akin to damming a river; the flow and course of energy is altered. The usual course of action is to refrain from working magic at these times, but that only applies to outward projections as these can go unexpectedly awry, like trying to navigate the waters of a storm-tossed sea. The older view of eclipses was one of great fear and foreboding. Inner work or spells cast on the self can still be done without difficulties, as deeper levels can remain intact despite any energetic turmoil above.

Whichever viewpoint you feel drawn to, it is best to take great care with the magic you decide to perform; either way, the eclipse is a time of great effect. Some believe a lunar eclipse is a good time to connect with crone goddesses, especially those connected to the moon.

The Blue Moon

Similarly to the new moon, a blue moon can be defined in a few different ways. One definition is if a full moon occurs twice in the same month, the *second* one is known as a blue moon; another definition has it that the *first* of the two is the blue moon. Another method of determining a blue moon is an astrological way; whenever a full moon occurs twice in the same astrological sign (which may not happen within the same calendar month), this too can be called a blue moon. And as if it weren't complicated enough, an old definition of "blue moon" is the third full moon in a season that has four full moons. No matter the definition, a blue moon affords us the opportunity to reassess matters; we get to double check, redo, or enhance any work done at the first full moon. This gives us an added dimension of power and depth that can aid our development spiritually and magically.

If you pre-plan, you can use the first moon and the subsequent moon to work long-term magic where you cast an initial spell and then later boost it with more magic. It helps to reserve the same items used in the initial spell to be used in the follow-up spell, keeping consistent with the moon's energetic return.

Simmering Potpourris

Here is a potpourri to fill your home with lunar energies.

LUNAR SPICE POTPOURRI

2 lemons, sliced (purification, love, moon magic)

3 cinnamon sticks (spirituality, love, success)

½ teaspoon cloves (love, money, protection, banishing)

Water

Fill a pot half full with water and add the remaining ingredients. Simmer on the stove for as long as desired, adding more water if needed.

Brews

Although milk, white wine, or plain white grape juice can be used as the ritual beverage for moon work, I like to use a specially crafted potion designed to align with and capture the essence of lunar energy.

Lunar Light Potion

1 cup water (moon work, blessing)

1 cup club soda (releasing energy)

1 cup white grape juice (moon work, abundance)

½ cup cucumber, sliced (moon work, healing)

1 lemon, sliced (moon work, purification)

In a clear jar with a tight-fitting lid, combine the water with the lemon and cucumber slices. The night before the full moon, place the jar in a window that faces the moon to allow the water to soak up the lunar rays, removing it before sunrise. Store the moon-infused water in the refrigerator until needed later that night. Just before serving, strain the moon water and add it to the grape juice. Slowly pour in the club soda and charge with the desire that this potion will help to connect you to the energies of the moon.

Incense

This incense is ritually appropriate for all phases of moon magic.

Esbat Incense

1 tablespoon thyme (healing, purification)

1 tablespoon rosemary (protection)

½ teaspoon poppy seeds (moon work)

¼ teaspoon coconut flakes, unsweetened
  (moon work)

Combine the ingredients and burn during any lunar-centric working.

Oils

These oil formulas are tailored to the main phases of the moon and the eclipses. Each of these oils should ideally be made during their respective lunar phases and charged with the energy of that time.

NEW MOON OIL

This oil mixture offers energy for a wide variety of intentions and is perfect for the burgeoning power of the new moon.

1 tablespoon white raisins (abundance)

1 teaspoon poppy seeds (love, money)

2 teaspoons turmeric (purification, fertility)

½ cup soy oil (protection)

Make in the usual way by warming all ingredients in a pot over low heat until you can smell the herbs in the air.

Dark Moon Oil

This dark moon formula is useful for work during the waning moon as well; it draws upon the deeper introspective nature of this part of the moon cycle.

¼ teaspoon vanilla extract (energy enhancer)

1 teaspoon cinnamon (spirituality)

1 teaspoon ginger (empowerment)

1 teaspoon rosemary (purification)

½ cup almond oil (wisdom)

Make the oil in the usual way, being sure to add the vanilla extract after the oil has cooled.

Full Moon Oil

2 teaspoons lemon peel (purification)

1 teaspoon poppy seeds (love)

1 teaspoon cucumber seeds (healing)

½ cup grape seed oil (abundance)

Heat the oil in the usual way. If you have a piece of silver available (such as an old earring) you can add it to the finished bottle of oil, but this is an optional power boost and not necessary.

LUNAR ECLIPSE OIL

1 teaspoon coconut flakes (protection)

2 tablespoons lettuce heart, chopped (rest)

½ cup soy oil (protection)

Make in the usual way as close to the time before the eclipse as you can.

SOLAR ECLIPSE OIL

1 tablespoon lemon peel (purification)

1 tablespoon orange peel (luck)

1 teaspoon turmeric (purification)

¼ teaspoon cayenne pepper (hex breaking)

¼ cup soy oil (protection)

¼ cup olive oil (healing, peace)

Make in the usual way before the eclipse.

BLUE MOON OIL

1 tablespoon lemon peel (moon work, purification)

1 tablespoon potato "eyes" (moon work, healing, growth)

1 small mushroom, sliced (psychic awareness)

½ cup soy oil (psychic awareness, protection)

Make in the usual way to promote growth and reassessing of projects.

Powders

The powder formula given here is an all-purpose moon powder. In some traditions cornmeal, wheat flour, or salt are used to draw magical symbols and this special powder can be used for this purpose. It can also be used to encircle candles or charms in order to further empower them during spell-casting.

Moon Dust Powder

2 tablespoons instant mashed potato flakes
(healing, moon work)

2 tablespoons coconut flakes, unsweetened
(moon work, protection)

2 tablespoons soy flour (psychic awareness,
protection)

Place all of the ingredients in a coffee grinder or food processor and grind into a powder. Charge with the energy of the moon and bottle for use.

Charms

To create a shining light infused with lunar energy that acts as a mystical beacon to the forces of spirit needn't be hopelessly complicated; a quick trip to any supermarket will provide us whatever need.

FULL MOON JAR CANDLE

Aside from becoming the perfect full moon esbat candle, the items used also correspond to cleansing and purification and can thus serve a dual purpose. In addition to the ingredients, you will also need an old pot, a sturdy knife, a spoon, and a small jar such as a jelly jar. All of these things should be items you no longer use for cooking. You may also need some paper towels. The candles called for are usually found in a store's utility or home goods aisle, or sometimes they're by the air fresheners.

1 box of white "household candles"

Coconut extract

1 teaspoon lemon zest (dried)

1 quarter-sized piece of dried lemon
     peel (a flat circle)

2 tablespoons white raisins

Pot or double boiler

It is a good idea to cover your workspace with newspaper or old plastic bags to catch any drippings or mess. Carefully cut the wax off of several of the candles, trying to preserve at least one of the wicks. Fill the jar with the wax pieces to overflowing to measure how much wax you will need. When you have accumulated the desired amount of wax bits, pour them into the pot (but don't heat it yet). Using the point of the knife, carefully pierce through the center of the dried lemon peel to make a small hole. Thread the wick through the hole and tie it in a knot. This will be the weight for the wick. Make sure that the wick is long enough to extend above the top of your jar.

Once the wick is prepared, place it in the center of the jar and sprinkle the white raisins over and around it to keep it in place. Now it is time to melt the wax. Placing the pot or double boiler on the stove over very low heat, stir the wax slowly to melt it; wax is flammable so caution is needed here. For safety, you can fill a clean can with the wax and place this in a pot of water, heating it until the wax melts. When it is melted (don't rush this step), remove it from the heat and add the dried lemon zest and the coconut extract. Stir to blend and the slowly pour enough of the wax to cover the raisins. Allow this to cool as this will ensure that the wick is firmly anchored in place. Once cooled, reheat the pot of wax and pour in another layer, holding the wick straight if necessary. If the wick is long enough, you can secure it to a pencil resting across the top of the jar and pour the full amount of wax in at one time. Allow the wax to harden. When the wax has hardened, there will usually be a depression formed in the surface. This is caused by a small pocket of air. To fix this, break through the surface with the knife to expose the air pocket and pour in a little more melted wax, just enough to create an even surface. Allow it to harden a second time, charge with your intent—in this case to connect with lunar energy and/or deities—and the candle is complete.

Foods

Though crescent-shaped cookies are a traditional food option during moon rituals, in my practice I like to make a standard post-ritual meal of Scottish stovies and bannock. The stovies are a mixture of potatoes and onion that are steam-cooked on the stove and the ingredients are aligned with moon work. The bannock bread is ritually appropriate but also made more so by creating a triple moon symbol on top of the loaf.

SCOTTISH STOVIES

6 potatoes (moon work, healing)

1 onion, yellow (healing)

Salt (blessing)

Pepper (protection)

1 tablespoon butter (transformation)

Water (blessing)

Peel the potatoes and slice them about ¼" thick. Peel and coarsely chop the onion. Mix the potatoes and onion together in a bowl and season with salt and pepper to taste. In a heavy saucepan, pour water in the bottom (approximately ¼-inch across the surface) and add the butter. Pour the potato/onion mixture into the pan and cover. Cook on medium heat, stirring occasionally and adding water if necessary to keep them burning, for about 30 minutes (until the potatoes are fork-tender and most of the liquid has been absorbed).

This basic recipe can be adapted in many ways. For vegans, butter can easily be omitted. For meat eaters, a half cup of cooked beef or sausage can be added on top of the potatoes while cooking. Optional moon-oriented vegetable add-ins include cauliflower, rutabaga, and turnips.

TRIPLE MOON BANNOCK

2 cups flour (abundance)

2 teaspoons baking powder (blessing)

½ teaspoon salt (blessing, cleansing)

½ cup milk (moon work, healing, protection)

2 tablespoons butter (transformation)

½ cup water

Biscuit cutter or glass

Oil for cooking

Medium-sized frying pan (9.5- to 10-inch pan)

Combine the water and milk in a large cup. Cream the butter, salt, baking powder, and a little bit of the flour together and slowly add the water/milk mixture, whisking together to blend. Add the flour to form a dough. Carefully press the dough into an oiled frying pan, to fill the pan like a large disk. Using the biscuit cutter or a drinking glass, press a circle into the middle of the dough to represent the full moon. Angling the cutter, make a "(" impression to the right of the circle and a ")" impression to the left, creating a triple crescent shape. Cook over low heat for approximately 10 minutes on each side so that it cooks all the way through and turns golden brown on the outside. Remove from heat and cool on a wire rack before serving.

Bath Salts

This bath salt can be used in the pre-ritual bath before lunar rituals.

Blessing of the Moon Bath Salt

1½ cups sea salt

¾ cup Epsom salt

¼ cup baking soda

1 teaspoon coconut extract (moon
    work, protection)

1 teaspoon lemon extract (moon
    work, purification)

Mix the dry ingredients and then add the extracts. Stir together and charge with the energies of blessing, purification, and lunar connection.

Ritual

This rite is an all-purpose lunar ritual that can be adapted depending on intent; simply substitute the correct oil, candle colors, and so on. This ritual can be used for any of the lunar phases or as a preliminary rite for any working. It is phrased in non-denominational terms though it can easily be adjusted to specific deities and traditions.

RITE OF ESBAT

2 white candles

Moon oil (type chosen based on lunar phase)

Cup of Lunar Light potion (or white wine)

Athame

Esbat incense

Incense charcoal

Cauldron, or incense burner

Bowl of salted water

Chosen meal

Prepare an altar in the center of the ritual area with all the things you will need for the rite. Light the candles and the incense. When you are ready, pick up the athame and energetically encircle yourself so that you are within a magical orb. Sprinkle saltwater around the circle in a clockwise direction to neutralize any energies not in harmony with your work. Afterward, settle yourself before the altar and meditate on the moon. In your mind's eye, see the moon floating above in its current phase, carrying all that power of this time. Reach out with your feelings and try to connect to the lunar energy and the divine energies above and behind the power of the moon.

When you feel a connection, pick up the cup of potion and the athame. Bless the potion (or wine) by lowering the tip of the athame into the cup and saying:

Vessel of creation, elixir of life,
union of spirit and flesh combine;
liquid charged through cup and knife,
pierce the veil and bless the wine.
Deities of the moon, through the power of all,
I call to you to lend your strength
and forge a greater bond.
Blessed be the union. Blessed be the voyage.
Blessed be the magic. Blessed be the power of all.

Raise the cup in both hands in gratitude, and drink in the energy of magic and communion. This infuses your body with magic. Now is the time to cast any spells, work any divinations, or call to any specific deities. Once the work has been completed, it is time to move to the ritual meal. Circle each serving plate of food with the athame in an act of energetic blessing saying, "May this food be blessed to nurture our bodies, minds, and spirits." After the meal is complete, it is time to conclude the rite.

Thank any deities you have called and draw back the circle through the athame by walking counterclockwise around the boundary. Extinguish the incense and the candles. The esbat is complete.

Witchy Ways

When I was younger, I could tell you what phase, astrological sign, and approximate location in the sky the moon was in at any given time. I adore the moon and before all of the business of adulthood took hold, I always kept very close to the lunar tides. Now, all the hustle and bustle of a busy life have made it necessary for me to remind myself of a great many things. I always have a list on hand and one of my pet sayings is (once I put an event in my phone calendar), "okay, it exists now" because if it isn't in my phone, it's not in my brain.

If you have a similarly busy life, it might be helpful to look up the full moons and any other significant celestial or astrological dates and add them into your cell phone's calendar as reminders. This way, you'll always be informed when the moon is full. I know that sounds weird (looking up at the sky could tell you), but being in the car or indoors so much, many of us rarely get the chance to "check in" with the moon and stars regularly. Having a reminder gives us the opportunity to stop and make that connection.

Lunar Shopping List

- Almond oil

- Baking powder

- Baking soda

- Butter

- Candles, white

- Cayenne pepper

- Cinnamon

- Cloves

- Club soda

- Coconut extract

- Coconut flakes, unsweetened

- Cucumber

- Epsom salt

- Flour, wheat

- Ginger

- Grape juice, white

- Grape seed oil

- Lemon extract

- Lemons

- Lettuce

- Mashed potato flakes, instant
- Milk
- Mushrooms
- Olive oil
- Onions
- Oranges
- Pepper, black
- Poppy seeds
- Potatoes
- Raisins, white
- Rosemary
- Salt
- Soy flour
- Soy oil
- Thyme
- Turmeric
- Vanilla extract

February 29

Whether we are seeking to shift away from the usual paradigm or trying to restore the balance to what has gone askew, Leap Day, February 29, is the ideal moment to act. An astronomical year—that is, the time it takes for the earth to make a complete orbit around the sun—is roughly 365 days and 6 hours, so to make up for the discrepancy in the calendar year, an extra day is added every four years in order to restore the balance and keep the calendar accurate.

Though this added day does not necessarily carry any inherently special magical power (other than what is present every other day) like a solstice or equinox does, it is still a powerfully symbolic day that can be magically harnessed to bring intentional change. Some of the old lore about this day includes the notion that women can propose to men on this day.[21] Though to the modern mind that sounds laughably sexist and ridiculous, in the Middle Ages, it was unheard of to operate outside of the strict societal mores. The idea was that February 29 exists outside of the usual calendar and thus was beyond the typical rules of conduct.

If we are free to act outside the normal boundaries, this is an ideal time to the break bonds we believe hold us down. It is also a good time to create dynamic change. If the history of this day is about upending social norms, why not harness it magically in spells designed for progressive social change?

Incense

Here is the incense formula for the Leap Day spell for change.

---

21 Nigel Pennick, *The Pagan Book of Days* (Rochester, VT: Destiny Books, 2001), 45.

Leap Day Incense

1 tablespoon sage (wishes)

1 tablespoon marjoram (all-purpose)

Combine the herbs and charge with the intent that it will manifest your wishes.

Oils

This is the oil recipe for the Leap Day spell for change featured below.

Leap Day Oil

1 tablespoon kale (balance)

2 teaspoons coffee (energy)

1 teaspoon nutmeg (mental ability)

½ cup soy oil

Warm all the ingredients until you can smell it in the air. Remove from heat and allow to cool. Strain the oil, charge, and bottle for use.

Ritual
Leap Day of Change

2 white candles

Leap Day incense

Leap Day oil

Incense charcoal

Cauldron

Paper and pen

Write what you wish to change (write the solution, not the problem) on a piece of paper. Anoint the corners of the paper with the oil. Anoint each candle with the oil, from both ends to the middle, and light the incense in the cauldron. Visualize what you want to occur and when this vision is at its peak, light the paper in the flame of one candle, drop it into the cauldron over the incense, and say:

> *Day out of time, this change I implore;*
> *a new shift in paradigm, is in store;*
> *what does not work shall cease to be,*
> *replaced with new path to see.*
> *For good of all and by free will,*
> *let this magic be fulfilled.*

Extinguish the candles and the incense.

Leap Day Shopping List
- Candles, white
- Coffee
- Kale
- Marjoram

- Nutmeg
- Sage
- Soy oil

Afterword

It was my intention when writing this book to show that magic exists everywhere, not only in far-off, mystical lands but as close as your local supermarket. All the items we use on a daily basis have magical energy. Their power often goes unnoticed due to their humble status. For example, cinnamon is easy to come by in our modern age, but a few centuries ago it was a rare, exotic spice for much of the world. The same holds true for most of the spices we take for granted today as well as a lot of the vegetables.

When I first began practicing kitchen-oriented magic, it was quite eye-opening to learn how truly exotic some of the most ordinary foods used to be. In general, it is important to look at the world with fresh eyes every now and then; it helps us gain greater insight, and that in turn empowers our magic even more. Happy shopping.

This section contains the tables of correspondence for all the herbs and foods used in this book plus many more additional items. A list of colors and their magical qualities is also included for handy reference.

Appendix 1:
Color Correspondences

Black: drawing in energy, dissolving illness or negativity, protection, multipurpose, Pluto energy

White: sending out energy, purification, protection, air, Uranus energy

Red: strength, passion, courage, protection, fire, Mars energy

Orange: communication, energy, change in accordance with will, Mercury energy

Yellow: intellect, divination, learning, persuasion, air, clear bright yellow can substitute for gold, Sun energy

Green: growth, fertility, healing, abundance, love (color of Venus), plants, earth energy

Blue: happiness, peace, soothing, water, Jupiter energy

Indigo: psychic ability, Saturn energy

Violet: spirituality, meditation, higher power

Brown: earth, animals, Saturn energy

Gray: neutrality, stalemate, clear light gray can substitute for silver

Silver: Goddess energy, dreams, moon magic, intuition, moon energy

Gold: God energy, strength, sun magic, success, prosperity, sun energy

Copper: love (again, tied to Venus), beauty

Pink: love, friendship, emotional healing, Venus energy

Opalescent colors: Neptune energy

Appendix 2:
Ingredient Table of Correspondences

Here is a listing of vegetables, herbs, fruits, grains, and other ingredients found in the supermarket. Not all of these are used in recipes in this book, but I have chosen to include as complete a listing of items as possible for easy reference when you want to create your own mixtures. You can also discover the magical potential of other recipes found in ordinary cookbooks or online.

Each ingredient is listed by name with corresponding element, planet, polarity, and magical uses included; some items have more than one association. The polarities listed will be along the yin/yang axis which I find less limiting than the "masculine/feminine" dynamic frequently used in herbal reference works. Not every listing contains information on planet, element, or polarity. This is because some items have a universal alignment.

Ingredient	Element	Planet	Polarity	Magical Uses
Agave	Fire	Mars	Yang	lust, love
Alfalfa	Earth	Venus	Yin	money, poverty protection
Allspice	Fire	Mars	Yang	money, luck, healing
Almond (nut and oil)	Air	Mercury	Yang	money, prosperity, wisdom
Anise	Air	Jupiter, Pluto	Yang	protection, meditation, purification
Apple	Water	Venus	Yin	love, healing, faery magic
Apricot	Water	Venus	Yin	love
Arugula	Fire	Mars	Yang	purification, lust
Arrowroot	Fire	Mars	Yang	healing, purification
Artichoke	Fire	Mars	Yang	protection, strength
Asparagus	Fire	Mars, Jupiter	Yang	lust, fertility, dragon magic
Avocado	Water	Venus	Yin	love
Baking powder	Earth		Yin	cleansing, blessing
Baking soda	Earth		Yin	cleansing, blessing
Banana	Water	Venus	Yin	fertility, prosperity
Barley	Earth	Venus	Yin	love, protection

Ingredient	Element	Planet	Polarity	Magical Uses
Basil	Fire	Mars, Pluto	Yang	love, banishing, wealth
Bay leaf	Fire	Sun	Yang	clairvoyance, purification, protection
Bean	Air	Mercury	Yang	protection, banishing
Beet	Earth	Saturn	Yin	love
Blackberry	Water	Venus	Yin	healing, protection, money
Blueberry	Earth	Venus	Yin	protection, warding
Brazil nut	Air	Mercury	Yang	love, fertility
Broccoli	Earth	Saturn	Yin	strength, empowerment
Brussels sprout	Water	Moon	Yin	protection, luck
Buckwheat	Earth	Venus	Yin	protection, prosperity
Butter	Earth	Moon	Yin	faery work, transformation
Cabbage	Water	Moon	Yin	luck, moon work
Cantaloupe	Water	Sun	Yang	healing, protection
Caraway	Air	Mercury	Yang	protection, lust
Cardamom	Water	Venus	Yin	love, lust
Carob	Fire	Jupiter	Yang	protection
Carrot	Fire	Mars	Yang	lust, fertility
Cashew	Fire	Sun	Yang	prosperity

Ingredient	Element	Planet	Polarity	Magical Uses
Catsup	Water	Venus	Yin	attraction, summoning
Cauliflower	Water	Moon	Yin	moon work, protection
Cayenne	Fire	Sun	Yang	hex breaking, passion
Celery	Fire, Water	Mercury	Yang	passion, mental clarity, calm
Chamomile	Water	Sun, Neptune	Yang	sleep, peace, money, love
Cheese	Earth	Saturn	Yang	success, happiness, transformation
Cherry	Water	Venus	Yin	fertility, love, divination
Chestnuts	Fire	Jupiter	Yang	success, love, strength
Chervil	Air	Mercury	Yin	spirit contact, wisdom, repels evil
Chicory	Air	Sun	Yang	luck, favor, frugality
Chili pepper	Fire	Mars	Yang	hex breaking, passion
Chives	Fire	Mars	Yang	banishing, protection
Chocolate	Fire	Mars	Yin	prosperity, love
Cinnamon	Fire	Sun	Yang	spirituality, love, success
Citron	Air	Sun	Yang	healing, psychic power

Ingredient	Element	Planet	Polarity	Magical Uses
Clove	Fire	Jupiter	Yang	banishing, protection, love, money
Club soda	Water	Moon	Yin	releasing energy, uniting elements
Coconut	Water	Moon	Yin	protection, moon magic
Coffee	Fire, Water	Mars, Neptune	Yin	energy, clarity, divination
Coriander (cilantro)	Fire	Mars	Yang	love, lust, healing
Corn	Earth	Venus	Yin	luck, protection
Cranberry	Fire, Water	Mars, Venus	Yin	protection, love, wine substitute
Cucumber	Water	Moon	Yin	healing, fertility, moon magic
Cumin	Fire	Mars	Yang	anti-theft, protection, banishing
Curry	Fire	Mars	Yang	protection (actual curry leaf, not the spice mix)
Date	Air	Sun	Yang	fertility, protection
Dill	Fire	Mercury	Yang	money, lust, protection
Dragon fruit	Water	Moon	Yin	psychic awareness
Dulse (red seaweed)	Water	Moon	Yin	moon magic, sea magic, lust

Ingredient	Element	Planet	Polarity	Magical Uses
Eggs	Earth	Moon	Yin	fertility, rejuvenation
Endive	Air	Jupiter	Yang	lust, love
Fennel	Fire	Mercury, Uranus	Yang	protection, healing, purification
Fig	Fire	Jupiter	Yang	fertility, protection, love
Flax	Fire	Mercury	Yang	money, protection, healing
Garlic	Fire	Mars	Yang	protection, banishing, healing
Gelatin	Earth			binding, sealing
Ginger	Fire	Mars	Yang	power, love, money
Gourd	Water	Moon	Yin	protection, moon magic
Grape	Water	Moon	Yin	fertility, abundance, moon magic
Grapefruit	Fire	Jupiter, Saturn	Yang	purification, healing
Guarana	Fire	Uranus	Yin	healing, wishes
Guava	Water	Venus	Yin	purification
Hazelnut (filbert)	Air	Sun	Yang	wisdom, protection, luck
Hibiscus (tea)	Water	Venus	Yin	lust, love

Ingredient	Element	Planet	Polarity	Magical Uses
Honey	Earth	Venus	Yin	love, binding, healing, prosperity
Horseradish	Fire	Mars	Yang	banishing, exorcism, purification
Huckleberry (can substitute for blueberry)	Water	Venus	Yin	purification, luck, hex breaking
Kale	Earth	Saturn	Yang	balance, dream magic, purification
Kelp	Water	Jupiter	Yin	protection, sea magic
Leek	Fire	Mars	Yang	protection, banishing, love
Lemon	Water	Moon	Yin	purification, love, moon magic
Lemongrass	Air	Mercury	Yang	psychic awareness
Lettuce	Water	Moon, Saturn	Yin	sleep, chastity, moon magic
Lime	Fire	Sun, Uranus	Yang	purification, healing, love
Mace (nutmeg)	Air	Mercury	Yang	divination, mental powers
Maple (syrup)	Air	Jupiter	Yang	love, healing, calm, binding
Marjoram (substitute with oregano)	Air	Mercury	Yang	love, protection, money, healing
Mayonnaise	Earth	Moon	Yin	success, money

Ingredient	Element	Planet	Polarity	Magical Uses
Milk (cow)	Earth	Moon	Yin	moon work, healing, protection
Milk (goat)	Earth	Moon	Yin	success, fertility, energy
Millet	Earth	Jupiter	Yang	money, luck, healing
Mint	Air	Mercury	Yang	money, healing, purification
Mushroom	Air	Mercury	Yang	psychic awareness, fertility, balance
Mustard	Fire	Mars	Yang	protection, purification, fertility
Nectarine	Water	Venus	Yin	love
Nutmeg	Air	Mercury	Yang	luck, money, love, healing
Oat	Earth	Venus	Yin	money, abundance
Olive (fruit and oil)	Fire	Sun	Yang	healing, peace, fertility, luck
Onion	Fire	Mars	Yang	protection, banishing, healing
Orange	Fire	Sun	Yang	love, luck, money
Oregano	Air	Mercury	Yang	love, protection, money, healing
Papaya	Water	Moon	Yin	love, protection, moon magic
Paprika (capsicum)	Fire	Mars	Yang	magical booster, creativity

Ingredient	Element	Planet	Polarity	Magical Uses
Parsley	Air	Mercury	Yang	purification, lust
Parsnip	Earth	Mars	Yang	sex magic
Pea	Earth	Venus	Yin	money
Peach	Water	Venus	Yin	love, fertility
Peanut	Fire	Sun Jupiter	Yang	money
Pear	Water	Venus	Yin	love
Pecan	Air	Mercury	Yang	money, prosperity
Pepper (black)	Fire	Mars	Yang	protection, banishing
Peppers	Fire	Mars	Yang	prosperity, protection
Persimmon	Water	Venus	Yin	luck, healing
Pimento	Fire	Mars	Yang	love
Pineapple	Fire	Sun	Yang	luck, money
Pine nut	Air	Mars	Yang	fertility, protection, money
Pistachio	Air	Mercury	Yang	hex breaking
Plum	Water	Venus, Saturn	Yin	love, protection
Pomegranate (fruit and juice)	Fire Protection	Mercury	Yang	luck, fertility
Poppy seed	Water	Neptune	Yin	moon work, love, money

Ingredient	Element	Planet	Polarity	Magical Uses
Potato	Earth	Moon	Yin	poppet, healing, moon work
Prune	Water	Venus	Yin	healing, love
Pumpkin	Earth	Moon	Yin	prosperity, healing, moon work
Quinoa	Fire	Sun	Yang	healing, fertility
Radish	Fire	Mars	Yang	protection, love, lust
Radicchio	Air	Sun	Yang	purification, luck
Raspberry	Water	Venus	Yin	love, protection
Rhubarb	Earth	Venus	Yin	healing, protection
Rice	Air	Sun	Yang	money, fertility, protection
Rosemary	Fire	Sun	Yang	purification, protection, love
Rutabaga	Earth	Moon	Yin	healing, moon work, protection
Rye	Earth	Venus, Pluto	Yin	love, protection
Saffron	Fire	Sun	Yang	love, healing, luck, strength
Safflower	Fire	Mars	Yang	divination, exorcism, hex breaking
Sage	Air	Jupiter	Yang	protection, money, cleansing

Ingredient	Element	Planet	Polarity	Magical Uses
Salt	Earth			purification, blessing, protection
Seaweed (bladderwrack, kelp)	Water	Moon	Yin	sea magic, protection, psychic work
Sesame (oil, seeds)	Fire	Sun	Yang	money, opportunity, lust
Shortening (lard)				base for salves
Soy	Earth	Moon	Yin	psychic awareness, protection
Spirits (distilled alcohol)	Fire	(Varies based on ingredients)		offering, spirituality, purification
Squash	Air	Moon	Yin	psychic ability, fertility, moon work
Star anise				psychic ability, protection, hex breaking
Stevia	Water	Jupiter	Yin	healing, success
Strawberry	Water	Venus	Yin	love, luck
Sugar	Water	Venus	Yin	love, purification
Summer savory	Air	Mercury	Yang	healing, love, lust
Sunflower (seeds and oil)	Air	Mercury	Yang	fertility, luck, strength

Ingredient	Element	Planet	Polarity	Magical Uses
Tarragon	Air	Venus	Yin	love, protection, purification
Tea	Fire	Sun	Yang	money, lust, courage
Thyme	Water	Venus	Yin	healing, energy, purification
Tobacco	Fire	Mars	Yang	purification, baneful herb substitute
Tomato	Water	Venus	Yin	protection, love, money
Turmeric	Water	Moon	Yin	purification, fertility, moon work
Turnip	Earth	Moon	Yin	protection, banishing
Vanilla	Water	Venus	Yin	love, energy, lust
Vinegar	Fire			purification, banishing, healing
Walnut	Fire	Sun	Yang	healing, strength
Watermelon	Water	Sun	Yang	purification, healing
Wheat	Earth	Venus	Yin	money, abundance, fertility
Wine (red)	Earth, Fire	Sun	Yang	luck, happiness, love, sun magic
Wine (white)	Earth, Water	Moon	Yin	luck, happiness, love, moon magic
Yogurt	Water	Moon	Yin	spirituality, creativity, moon magic
Zucchini	Earth	Jupiter	Yin	protection, prosperity

Bibliography

Blair, Briana. *The Herbal Magic Correspondences Guide.* Raleigh, NC: lulu.com, 2014.

Buckland, Raymond. *Scottish Witchcraft and Magick: The Craft of the Picts.* Woodbury, MN: Llewellyn Publications, 2006.

Cabot, Laurie. *Celebrate the Earth: A Year of Holidays in the Pagan Tradition.* New York: Delta, 1994.

———. *Laurie Cabot's Book of Shadows.* Salem, NH: Copper Cauldron Publishing, 2015.

———. *Power of the Witch: The Earth, The Moon and the Magical Path to Enlightenment.* New York: Delta, 1989.

Chambers, Robert. *The Book of Days: A Miscellany of Popular Antiquities in Connection With the Calendar,*

Including Anecdote, Biography and History, Curiosities of Literature, and Oddities of Human Life and Character. Charleston, SC: Nabu Press, 2010.

Cunningham, Scott. *The Magic in Food: Legends, Lore, and Spellwork.* St. Paul, MN: Llewellyn Publications, 1991.

———. *The Magical Household: Spells and Rituals for the Home.* St. Paul, MN: Llewellyn Publications, 2010.

Day, Christian *The Witches' Book of the Dead.* San Francisco: Weiser Books, 2011.

De Angeles, Ly. *When I See the Wild God: Encountering Urban Celtic Witchcraft.* St. Paul, MN: Llewellyn Publications, 2004.

———. *Witchcraft: Theory and Practice.* St. Paul, MN: Llewellyn Publications, 2005.

Dunwich, Gerina. *A Witch's Halloween: A Complete Guide to Magick, Incantations, Recipes, Spells and Lore.* Avon, MA: Provenance Press, 2007.

Farrar, Janet and Stewart Farrar. *The Witches Bible Compleat.* New York: Magickal Childe, 1984.

Grimassi, Raven. *Wiccan Magick: Inner Teachings of the Craft.* St. Paul, MN: Llewellyn Publications, 1998.

Grimassi, Raven. *The Witches' Craft: The Roots of Witchcraft and Magical Transformation.* St. Paul, MN: Llewellyn Publications, 2002.

Guest, Lady Charlotte. *The Mabinogion: Translated from the Red Book of Hergest.* Mineola, New York: Dover Publications, 1997.

Gwyn. *Light from the Shadows: Modern Traditional Witchcraft.* Taunton, UK: Capall Bann, 1999.

Hughes, Kristoffer. *The Journey into Spirit: A Pagan's Perspective on Death, Dying, and Bereavement.* Woodbury, MN: Llewellyn Publications, 2014.

Illes, Judika. *Encyclopedia of 5,000 Spells: The Ultimate Reference Book for the Magical Arts.* New York: HarperOne, 2004.

Lazic, Tiffany. *The Great Work: Self-Knowledge and Healing Through the Wheel of the Year.* Woodbury, MN: Llewellyn Publications, 2015.

Marquis, Melanie. *The Witch's Bag of Tricks: Personalize Your Magick and Kickstart Your Craft.* Woodbury, MN: Llewellyn Publications, 2011.

McColman, Carl. *366 Celt: A Year and a Day of Celtic Wisdom and Lore.* Newburyport, MA: Hampton Roads Publishing, 2008.

Meekins, Jeannie. *Saint Valentine: The Man Who Became the Patron Saint of Love.* n.p., LearningIsland.com, 2013.

O'Brien, Lora. *Irish Witchcraft from an Irish Witch.* Franklin Lakes, NJ: New Page Books, 2005.

Patterson, Rachel. *A Kitchen Witch's World of Magical Food.* New Alresford, UK: Moon Books, 2015.

Pennick, Nigel. *The Pagan Book of Days: A Guide to Festivals, Traditions and Sacred Days of the Year.* Rochester, VT: Destiny Books, 2001.

Rajchel, Diana. *Samhain: Rituals, Recipes and Lore for Halloween (Llewellyn's Sabbat Essentials).* Woodbury, MN: Llewellyn Publications, 2015.

Rich, Vivian A. *Cursing the Basil and other Folklore from the Garden.* Victoria, BC: Touchwood Editions, 2010.

Index